# PROJECT  REPORT

# RULES OF ENGAGEMENT
## OCTOBER 1972 - AUGUST 1973(U)
### 1 MARCH 1977

## PROJECT CHECO
## OFFICE OF HISTORY
## HQ PACAF

Prepared by:
CAPTAIN WILLIAM R. BURDITT

## SECURITY NOTICE

This is a TOP SECRET document and will be handled in accordance with DOD 5200.1-R and AFR 205-1. It contains information affecting the National Defense of the United States and, accordingly, utmost security will be afforded in the distribution and dissemination of its contents.

Reproduction is authorized to the extent necessary for accomplishing an official government function.

This document is classified TOP SECRET/NOT RELEASABLE TO FOREIGN NATIONALS to conform to the highest classification of the source documents.

In accordance with the provisions of DOD 5200.1-R and AFR 205-1, this volume is Excluded from the General Declassification Schedule of Executive Order 11652 on a derivative basis.

FOREWORD

The counterinsurgency and unconventional warfare environment of Southeast Asia (SEA) resulted in the employment of USAF airpower to meet a multitude of requirements. The varied applications of airpower involved nearly the full spectrum of USAF aerospace weapons, support equipment, and manpower. As a result, there has been an accumulation of operational data and experiences that has been collected and documented which must be analyzed for their current and future impact upon USAF policies, concepts, and doctrine.

Fortunately, the value of collecting and documenting our SEA experiences was recognized at an early date. In 1962, Hq USAF directed CINCPACAF to establish an activity that would be primarily responsive to Air Staff requirements and direction, and would provide timely, analytical studies of USAF combat operations in SEA.

Project CHECO, an acronym for Contemporary Historical Examination of Current Operations, was established to meet this Air Staff requirement. Managed by Hq PACAF, with elements formerly at Hq 7AF, 7/13AF, and 13ADVON, Project CHECO provides a scholarly, "on-going" historical examination, documentation, and reporting of USAF policies, concepts, and doctrine in PACOM. Since the drawdown in SEA, the Project CHECO functions have been centralized in the Office of PACAF History.

This CHECO report is part of the overall documentation and examination which has been accomplished. It is an authentic source for the assessment of the effectiveness of USAF airpower in PACOM when used in proper context. The reader must view the study in relation to the events and circumstances at the time of its preparation--recognizing that it was prepared on a contemporary basis which restricted perspective and that the author's research effort was limited to records available within his local headquarters area.

WILLIAM H. LANDIS, Colonel, USAF
Chief of Staff

## ABOUT THE AUTHOR

Captain William R. Burditt was commissioned in February 1968 upon completion of Officer Training School at Lackland AFB, Texas. He completed training in March 1969, attended pilot instructor training at Tyndall AFB, Florida, and instructed in the T-38 at Laughlin AFB, Texas, for over three years. His flying duties at Laughlin included those of a check pilot and wing standardization/evaluation officer. He also served as Chief, Information Division in the Wing Information Office for one year while at Laughlin AFB. He is a graduate of Southwest Texas Junior College with an A.A. in Pre-veterinary Medicine and of Texas A & M University with a B.S. in Animal Science. He completed squadron officer school by correspondence.

\*     \*     \*     \*     \*

The author's draft was reviewed by competent authorities; it was edited by Mr. Claude G. Morita, Hq PACAF/HO/CHECO.

CONTENTS

| | |
|---|---|
| FOREWORD | iii |
| ABOUT THE AUTHOR | iv |
| LIST OF ILLUSTRATIONS | vii |
| LIST OF OPERATING AUTHORITIES | vii |
| INTRODUCTION | 1 |
| I. OVERVIEW | 5 |
|     The Republic of Vietnam | 6 |
|     North Vietnam | 7 |
|     Laos | 9 |
|     Cambodia | 16 |
| II. REPUBLIC OF VIETNAM | 21 |
| III. NORTH VIETNAM | 33 |
| IV. LAOS | 45 |
| V. CAMBODIA | 73 |
| VI. SUMMARY | 91 |
| APPENDIX | 95 |
|   A. Southeast Asia Basic Rules of Engagement, Cease-fire in RVN and NVN, Effective 272359Z January 1973 | 95 |
|   B. Southeast Asia Basic Rules of Engagement, Cease-fire in NVN, RVN, the DMZ, and Laos | 103 |

C.  Southeast Asia Operating Authorities, Cease-fire in NVN, RVN, the DMZ, Laos, and Cessation of Combat Activities by U.S. Forces in GKR.................................... 111

D.  Southeast Asia Basic Rules of Engagement, Cease-fire in NVN, RVN, the DMZ, Laos, and Cessation of Combat Activities by U.S. Forces in GKR, Effective 150400Z August 1973.................................................. 121

NOTES............................................................. 127

GLOSSARY.......................................................... 137

DISTRIBUTION...................................................... 141

## LIST OF ILLUSTRATIONS

**Figure**

1. Route Packages and Restricted Areas........................ 10
2. Operating Areas in Laos................................... 12
3. Special Operating Areas and Raven Boxes in Laos........... 14
4. Freedom Deal, September 1972.............................. 18
5. DMZ and Cua Viet River.................................... 24
6. Laos PCA.................................................. 58
7. Restricted Areas in Freedom Deal.......................... 82
8. Expansion of Freedom Deal................................. 86

## LIST OF OPERATING AUTHORITIES

**Table**

1. Southeast Asia Operating Authorities--Cease-fire in the RVN and NVN (RVN)................................... 26
2. Southeast Asia Operating Authorities--Cease-fire in the RVN and NVN (NVN)................................... 42
3. Southeast Asia Operating Authorities--Cease-fire in the RVN and NVN (Laos).................................. 54
4. Operating Authorities--Laos............................... 62
5. Southeast Asia Operating Authorities--Laos................ 66
6. Southeast Asia Operating Authorities--Cease-fire in RVN and NVN (Khmer Republic)............................ 74

INTRODUCTION

(U) At the operational level, the rules of engagement (ROE) were the detailed set of rules which defined the limits of U.S. military operations in Southeast Asia (SEA). Since these rules originated at the highest U.S. governmental levels, they were essentially the expression of U.S. national policy on the battlefields of SEA. The ROE have been viewed by staff officers in several different contexts. The most prevalent was that they were excessively restrictive and prevented the field commanders from utilizing air power to its maximum effectiveness. From an operational viewpoint, the latter argument was compelling. However, when the ROE were viewed as the embodiment of national policy in waging a limited war, many of the limitations imposed on the use of air power not only seem reasonable but necessary. In yet another perspective, changes in the ROE were used to apply pressure on the North Vietnamese, prodding them to negotiate for ending the war in Vietnam. In his report to the Congress on 3 May 1973, President Richard M. Nixon explained:

(U) We resumed bombing (18 December 1972) north of the 20th parallel in North Vietnam, which we had suspended while serious negotiations were underway. We had to make clear that Hanoi could not continue to wage war in the south while its territory was immune and that we would not tolerate an indefinite delay in negotiation.[1]

(U) The ROE were changed or amended by air operating authorities (AOA) which were sent in message form from the Joint Chiefs of Staff (JCS) to the Commander in Chief, Pacific Command (CINCPAC). These messages essentially identified those military activities which could be conducted, the specific purposes for which they could be conducted, and, if required, the effective periods during which those activities would be authorized. The basic operating authorities and ROE, established and promulgated by the JCS through CINCPAC, were provided for action (along with additional guidance/restrictions) to the regional sub-unified command, either the Commander, U.S. Military Assistance Command, Vietnam (COMUSMACV), or Commander, U.S. Support Activities Group (COMUSSAG), for use by the Air Force component commander, Commander, Seventh Air Force (COM 7AF).* Additional operational

---

* (U) When Hq USSAG/7AF became operational on 15 February 1973, COMUSSAG was dual-hatted as COM 7AF.

guidance was provided by the various in-theater U.S. embassy staffs and, occasionally, from the Pacific Command (PACOM) component commanders. This guidance was conveyed through CINCPAC to COMUSMACV (later COMUSSAG) and then, along with any additional guidance/restrictions imposed by COMUSMACV (or COMUSSAG), to the COM 7AF to use in structuring the operational guidance for SEA air operations.[2]

(S) Initially, 7AF OPORD 71-17 (December 1971) was created to provide a consolidated, comprehensive document containing all-source operational rules for SEA operations.[3] The OPORD served its purpose well as long as the level of U.S. effort was relatively stable; however, as the North Vietnamese Army (NVA) general offensive built up momentum through the spring and summer of 1972, guidance on U.S. military operations began to change so rapidly in response to both battlefield conditions and negotiating efforts in Paris that the single document, the OPORD, could not be updated and expanded fast enough to reflect the full scope of current objectives. At this point, the precedent was established to maintain a standing Seventh Air Force ROE in published form providing general guidance, accompanied by a series of instructions -- in message form or as special instructions (SPINs) to the current fragmentary operations order (frag) to provide supplemental current ROE and AOA -- which were provided separately, even for day-to-day SEA operations. Longer term guidance and changes were issued by message format as quickly as possible as operational supplements to update the OPORD. ROE for short term or specifically "tailored" operations, such as Linebacker and Linebacker II, were not incorporated into OPORD 71-17, but were disseminated, maintained and amended by messages/SPINs.

CHAPTER I

OVERVIEW

(U)  This report is the fourth in a series of CHECO reports on the ROE, summarizing significant events and changes which occurred between October 1972 and August 1973. Throughout this period, the operating authorities formulated by the JCS were in most cases directly related to the peace negotiations conducted in Paris between the United States and the Democratic Republic of Vietnam (DRV). Consequently, this report accounts for changes in the ROE, chronologically, as they applied to the different areas of SEA: The Republic of Vietnam (RVN), North Vietnam (NVN), Laos, and Cambodia. This presentation not only provides the reader with significant changes in the ROE between October 1972 and August 1973, but also portrays the close relationship between national policy and the conduct of air operations in SEA. The intensity of bombing, the number of sorties authorized, and the territorial restrictions were constantly changed, particularly through January 1973. Specifically, they followed the negotiating trends and the sincerity, or the lack of it, with which the North Vietnamese approached peace negotiations. These negotiations culminated in the signing of the "Agreement on Ending the War and Restoring Peace in Vietnam" on 27 January 1973 in Paris. Because these changes would be less significant to the reader without some prior knowledge of the ROE, this chapter provides a brief summary of the ROE as they stood in September 1972.*

## The Republic of Vietnam

(S) The ROE in the RVN were basically applied to operations involving close air support (CAS) of ground forces. Consequently, the rules were formulated for the purpose of minimizing casualties to friendly forces and noncombatants, decreasing civilian property damage, and preventing short rounds.[4] This guidance, designed as it was to be proscriptive, dictated who could control air strikes and when a controlling agency was or was not required. Ordnance restrictions, ordnance jettison procedures, return of ground fire, search and rescue (SAR) missions, border control, and strike clearance authorities were also governed by the ROE. The rules covered the use of ordnance as it affected troops in contact (TIC) situations, uninhabited areas, inhabited

---

* (U) More detailed information on the ROE as they existed through September 1972 can be obtained from the CHECO Report, Rules of Engagement, November 1969-September 1972, dated 1 Mar 1973 and 7AF OPORD 71-17.

areas, urban areas, and areas of cultural value. Rules governing the use of specified strike zones (SSZ), the positive control zone (PCZ), and demilitarized zone (DMZ) were all specified in the ROE for RVN.[5]

(S) The last significant change in the ROE for the RVN occurred after the cessation of offensive air operations against NVN in 1968. It prohibited U.S. aircraft operating in South Vietnam from entering the DMZ except in hot pursuit of hostile aircraft or in immediate response to firings of surface-to-air missiles (SAM) and antiaircraft artillery (AAA). To counter a NVN force buildup in the DMZ, this restriction was later modified to allow tactical air support and B-52 strikes in the southern half of the DMZ.[6]

North Vietnam

(S) After the United States terminated offensive air operations against NVN in November 1968, the air campaign became pendulum-like, swinging back and forth in intensity as the force of opinion changed in Washington. In the early part of 1970, operations under the definition of "protective reaction strikes" were authorized which allowed strikes below 19 degrees north latitude in immediate response to enemy aircraft or

SAM/AAA threats to allied aircraft.[7] The restrictive strike authority continued to ease throughout 1970 and 1971 and began to include SAM sites, petroleum, oil, and lubricants (POL) storage areas as well as truck parks. However, these air strikes were required to be conducted below the 19th parallel.* In April 1972, the JCS again authorized tactical air operations in NVN up to 19 degrees north latitude under the nickname Freedom Train.[8] The restrictions on air operations continued to ease through April and on 9 May 1972, with President Nixon's announcement of the mining of North Vietnamese ports, offensive air operations throughout NVN were again authorized with the major objective to "reduce or restrict NVN assistance from external sources."[9] This marked the resumption of the interdiction bombing of NVN.

(S) The interdiction campaign, nicknamed Linebacker, was undertaken to bring sufficient pressure to bear on the government of NVN to compel it to stop its aggression and terminate its support of insurgent operations in South Vietnam, Laos, and Cambodia.

---

* (U) More detailed information on the protective reaction strikes can be obtained from CHECO report, <u>Rules of Engagement, November 1969-September 1972</u>, under the nicknames Freedom Bait, Louisville Slugger, Fracture Cross, Proud Deep Alpha, and Prize Bull.

Linebacker rules authorized TACAIR and B-52 strikes to destroy and disrupt enemy POL supplies, transportation resources, and lines of communication (LOCs). In addition, air operations were authorized to neutralize enemy defenses and carry on armed reconnaissance throughout NVN except certain restricted areas. These restricted areas included the People's Republic of China (PRC) buffer zone and areas within ten nautical miles (NM) of the center of Hanoi and Haiphong, although the JCS could validate targets within these areas.[10] Refer to Figure 1. Linebacker rules continued essentially unchanged through September 1972.

Laos

(TS) The U.S. goal in Laos was to support the neutrality of Laos and to hinder the infiltration of North Vietnamese men and supplies into South Vietnam over the Ho Chi Minh Trail in eastern Laos. The role of U.S. air power in support of this goal was the interdiction of NVN supply routes and CAS of Royal Lao forces against Laotian guerrillas during the dry season and the strategic bombing of the NVN staging areas and harassment of the roadwork crews during the wet season.[11]

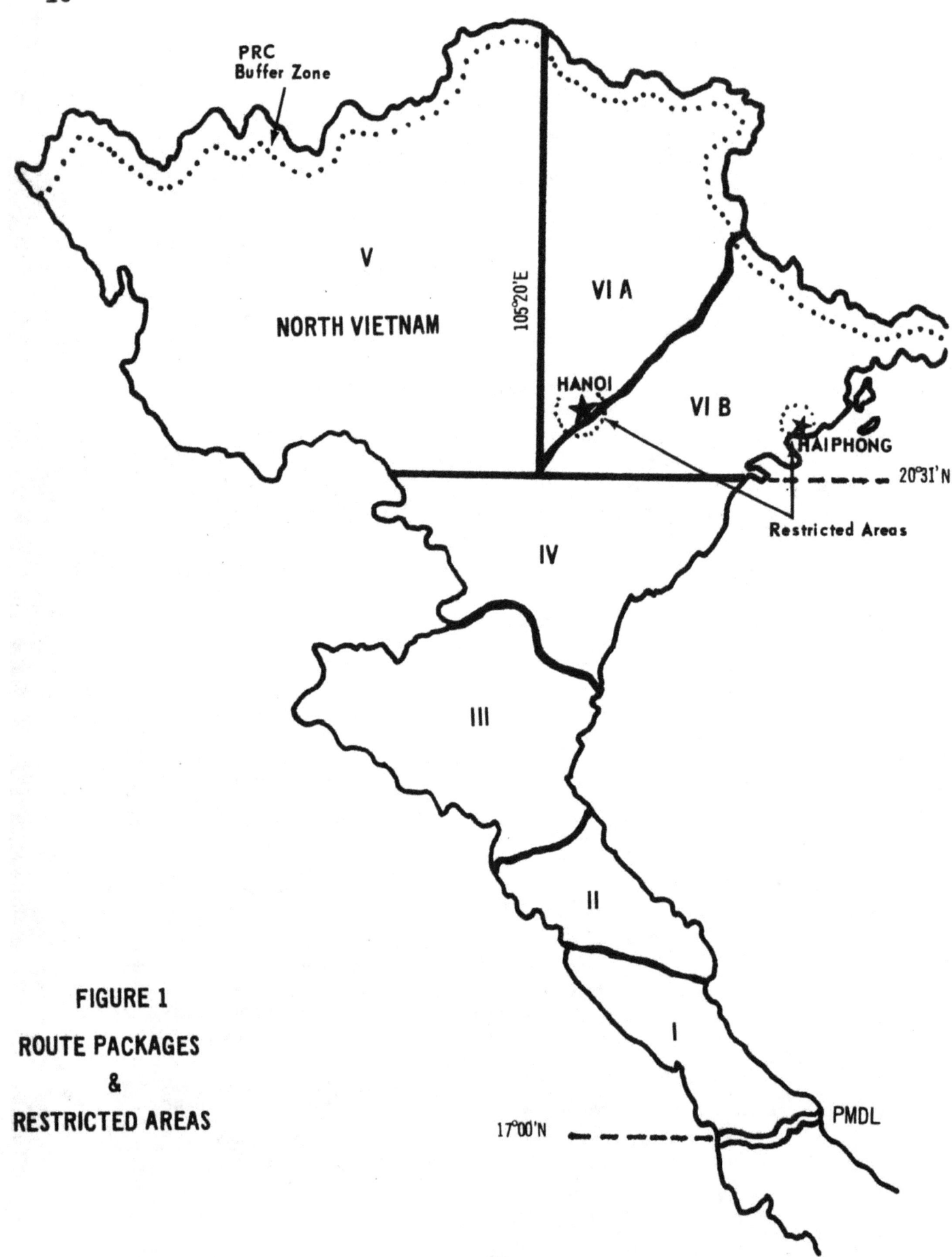

FIGURE 1
ROUTE PACKAGES & RESTRICTED AREAS

Because of the sensitivity of the U.S. involvement in Laos and because of the need to make the air support of U.S. goals in Laos compatible with various operational conditions, Laos was artificially partitioned into five operating areas, each of which had its own ROE. Refer to Figure 2 for the location of the operating areas. The first division separated the Laotian panhandle from the main part of the country. The southern panhandle was known as Steel Tiger (SL) while the remainder of Laos was identified as Barrel Roll (BR). Further divisions in each area resulted in two operating areas in SL, SL East and SL West, and three in BR, BR North, BR East, and BR West. The ROE in each area reflected the logic of the subdivision. BR North was a buffer zone between allied operating areas and the PRC. Any U.S. air strike or tactical air reconnaissance required JCS approval. The BR West and Steel Tiger West operating areas were similar to each other and had less restrictive ROE than BR North. Operations in these two areas were primarily for the purpose of assisting RLG forces in counterinsurgency (COIN) operations and area security. In general, all strikes, including the return of ground

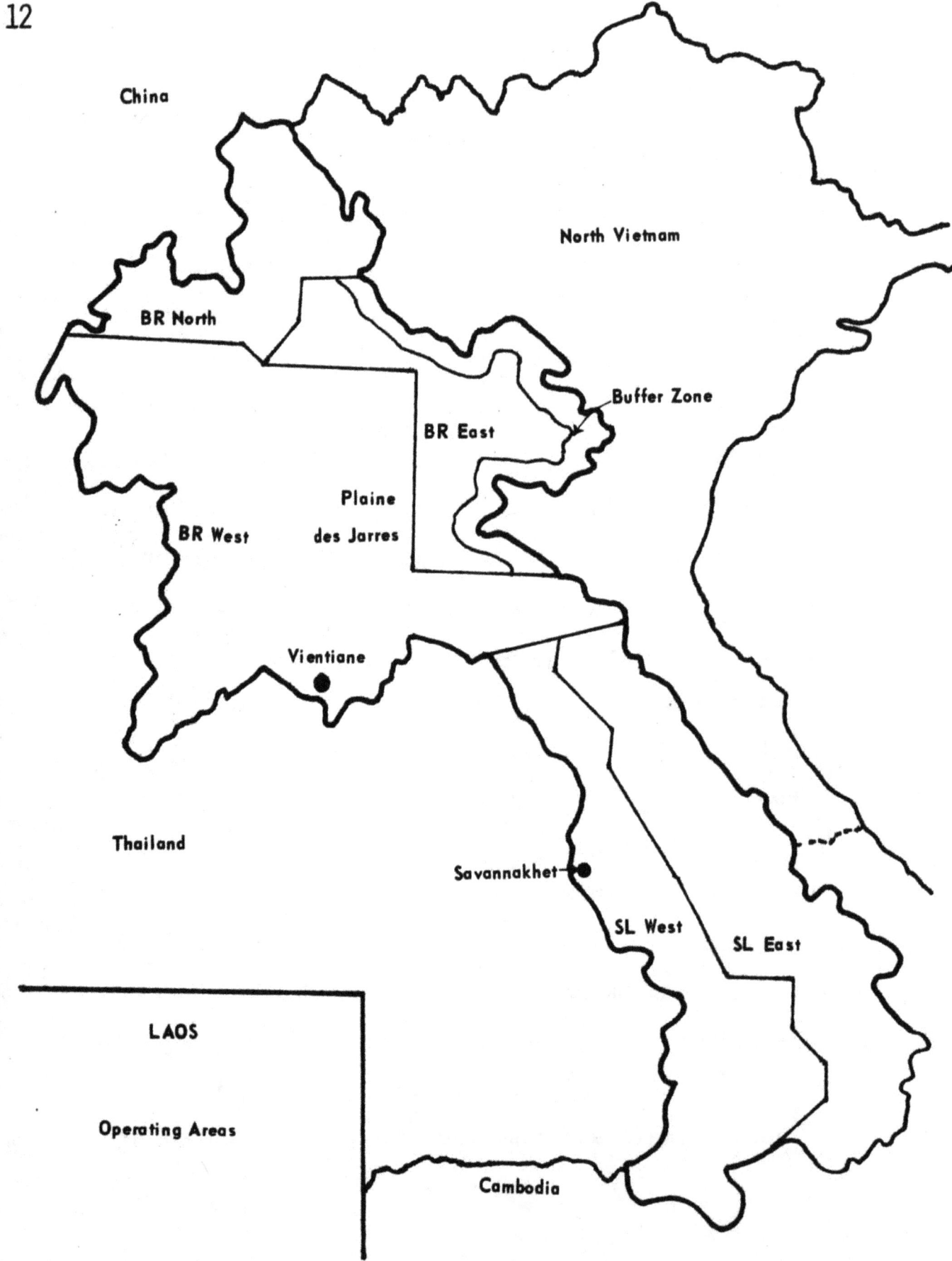

fire, had to be under forward air controller/forward air guide (FAC/FAG) control, accompanied by the approval of the JCS and the U.S. Ambassador to Laos. BR East and SL East had the least restrictive ROE because operations conducted there were geared to interdict massive movements of NVN troops, supplies and materiel through the Ho Chi Minh Trail in support of enemy initiatives in the RVN and Khmer Republic (GKR). Ground fire could be returned in these areas without FAC/FAG control within 200 meters of all LOCs, up to the ten nautical mile buffer zone. This buffer zone was along the NVN border in BR East.[12]

(S) As the ROE became less restrictive in NVN, the rules governing air operations in Laos followed suit. In 1970, the buffer zone in BR East was reduced to four nautical miles in width. As the interdiction campaign in NVN picked up in tempo in 1972, the restrictions existed in name only and the JCS authorized air strikes against all targets validated by the American Embassy (AmEmb) Vientiane until the termination of the Linebacker campaign in NVN. Although the BR East ROE became less restrictive, those in BR West were tightened. This

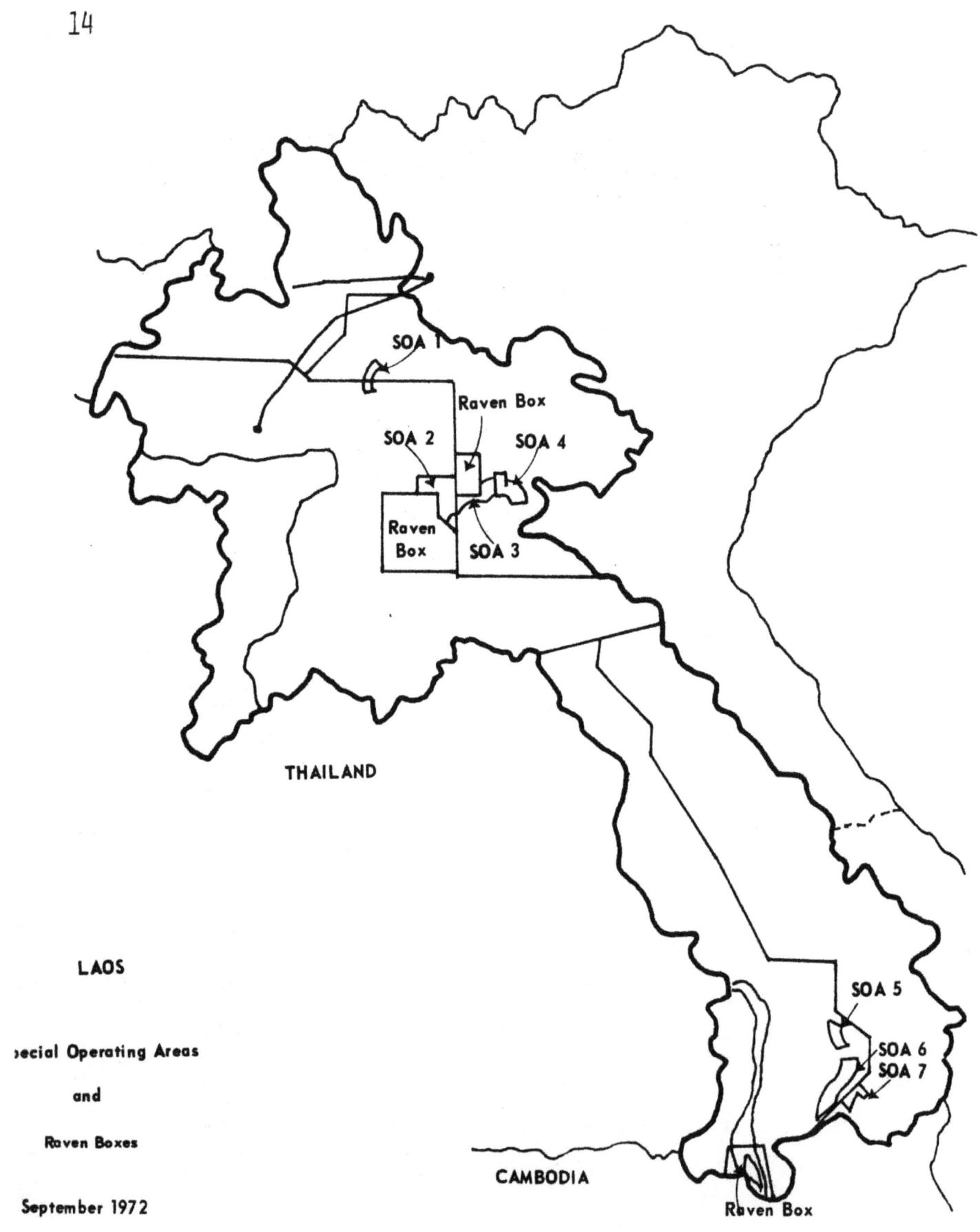

FIGURE 3

resulted because of concern over the possibility of an incident arising from the presence of Chinese construction crews who were engaged in building a road in Laos. This road began to cross from BR North into BR West. The JCS finally extended the restrictive BR North ROE to encompass all known or suspected Chinese positions in northern Laos.[13]

(S) An increase in the number of special operating areas* (SOAs) accompanied the ROE changes. In 1969, there were only two SOAs, located in BR East. By June 1972, this number had increased to seven. This increase in the number of SOAs and the gradual elimination of the BR East buffer zone were the most significant changes in the ROE of Laos for the period between 1970 and 1972. However, the appearance of the Raven Control Box[+] and the SOAs just north of the Cambodian border was evidence of the increased U.S. involvement in Cambodia.[14] Refer to Figure 3.

---

* (U) A special operating area was an area validated in advance by the AmEmb Vientiane for air strikes against all forms of enemy military activity which could be conducted without FAC control.

+ (S) A Raven control box was an area in which air strikes were under the control of a Raven FAC or FAG. FAGs and Laotian observers flying with Raven FACs had the AmEmb Vientiane authorization to validate targets of opportunity.

## Cambodia

(S) The United States became actively involved in the Khmer Republic on 1 May 1970, the beginning of the Cambodian incursion. As could be expected, the primary role of U.S. air power was in the support of ground troops. When the ROE first became effective in late May 1970, they were composed basically of two parts, those dealing with the Freedom Deal area and those affecting the rest of the country. The basic interdiction area, nicknamed Freedom Deal, was that part of Cambodia bounded by an imaginary line drawn 200 meters west of and equidistant from the Mekong to its west; along the Laotian border on the north; the RVN border on the east; and Route 13 on the south. The Freedom Deal area was modified on several occasions later, generally toward expanding it. The ROE in Freedom Deal were similar to those for South Vietnam. FACs could control all tactical air strikes except properly cleared, radar-controlled strikes. The Forces Armees Nationale Khmer (FANK) could validate all targets. Aircraft could return ground fire immediately if it did not originate in an urban area, town, village, or hamlet. If the hostile fire came from such a settled area, FANK approval was required before aircraft could return fire. Special operating areas were defined in which all targets were prevalidated by the FANK; aircraft could attack any enemy target without further approval. Strikes outside the Freedom Deal area required prior approval of the JCS.[15]

(S) Unique to the Cambodian ROE were prevalidated Category "A" and "B" LOCs, along which enemy targets could be struck without further approval. Category "A" LOCs were those along which there were no friendly personnel, traffic, installations, or dwellings. Aircraft could expend ordnance on targets or suspected targets within 1,000 meters (on either side) of a road or waterway. Area denial munitions were permitted. Category "B" LOCs were those used by friendlies as well as the enemy. Aircraft could strike motor vehicles or moving watercraft at night and motor-powered boats and vehicles during the day within 500 meters on either side of the LOC.

(S) By November 1970, the Freedom Deal interdiction area had been expanded to the west to encompass new enemy buildup areas; armed reconnaissance was permitted throughout the interdiction area. By the end of September

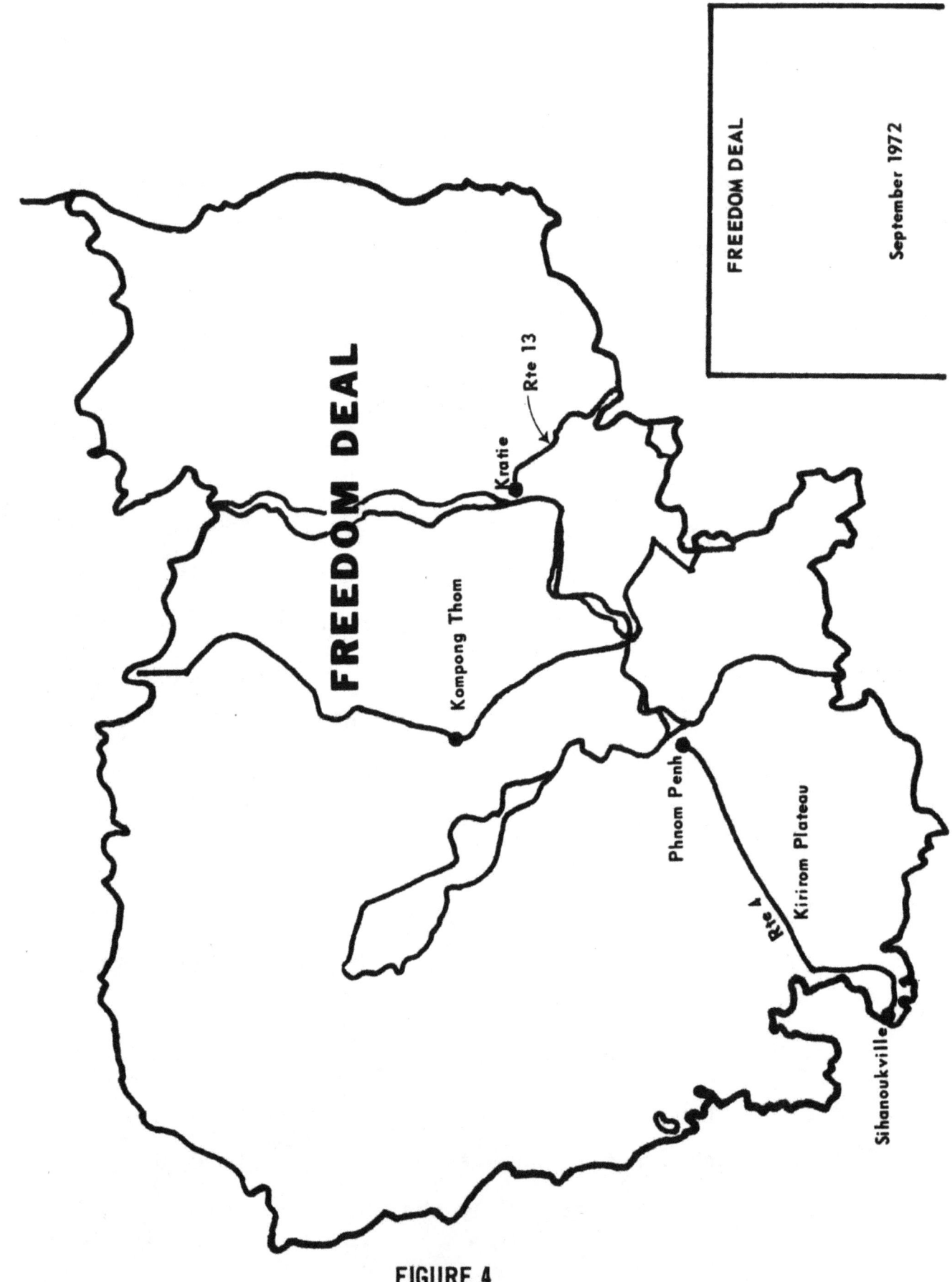

FIGURE 4

1972, the two basic areas of operation were still in effect. Freedom Deal, the interdiction area, encompassed the eastern one-third of the country and TACAIR, gunship, and B-52 interdiction strikes were authorized against enemy troops and supplies. Refer to Figure 4. In the rest of the country, Seventh Air Force had discretionary authority to employ TACAIR and gunship interdiction in any situation that posed a threat to major Khmer positions.[16]

## CHAPTER II

## REPUBLIC OF VIETNAM

(TS) As in the past, the ROE in the RVN were mainly concerned with close air support of ground forces. The ROE were to remain the same in this area, but as the prospect of a possible cease-fire became clearer, the cross-border operations were again subject to changes relative to the Paris peace negotiations. The first large-scale revision of the ROE came on 30 October 1972 when the JCS sent CINCPAC a number of operating authorities which affected the air activities in and adjacent to the RVN. In an effort to forcefully diminish the North Vietnamese buildup just north of and within the DMZ, the use of ground forces, naval gunfire, and TACAIR was authorized on 30 October to counter this threat and could be used until the enemy weapons and artillery support facilities were neutralized. In the case of SAM or AAA firing at allied aircraft from across or within the DMZ, an immediate protective reaction was authorized to neutralize these weapons, installations, and immediate supporting facilities.[17]

Although the prospects of a cease-fire -- realistic for the first time -- brought about more action by both sides to secure key points prior to the actual cease-fire taking place, JCS approval was still required for counteractions against a major ground or air attack across the DMZ.

Search and rescue (SAR) operations for U.S. personnel could still be conducted throughout SEA. However, the operating authorities prohibited SAR efforts for other allied aircrews in NVN. The use of riot control agents (RCA) and the return of ground fire were authorized in the RVN when necessary to protect the SAR force and insure the recovery of personnel.[18]

When it became evident in November that the North Vietnamese were not seriously pursuing peace negotiations, the JCS extended the 30 October operating authorities from 1 December to 31 December.[19] In connection with this extension, intelligence reports indicated a major enemy campaign to move supplies and equipment into South Vietnam as well as plans to launch a new offensive into Military Region (MR) I, prompting the JCS to authorize the maximum use of both TACAIR and B-52s between the DMZ and the Cua Viet River just north of Quang Tri. Refer to Figure 5. This use of air power was to remain in effect for a 48-hour period after which a maximum TACAIR/B-52 effort was to be initiated against suspected enemy logistic and manpower buildups throughout the RVN and Route Package I.[20]

(U) The stalemate at the peace table caused by the lack of sincere negotiations by the North Vietnamese continued into December 1972. It was evident that Hanoi was stalling for time and these tactics brought out some strong opposition in Saigon about the proposed peace settlement. In order to provide an incentive for the DRV to continue meaningful negotiations, it was plain to U.S. strategists that strong action was needed. On 18 December, U.S. bombing north of the 20th parallel was resumed. President Nixon later explained what had occurred:

> The more difficult Hanoi became, the more rigid Saigon grew. There was a danger that the settlement which was so close might be pulled apart by conflicting pressures. We decided to bring home to both Vietnamese parties that there was a price for continuing the conflict.... We had to make clear that Hanoi could not continue to wage war in the south while its territory was immune, and that we would not tolerate an indefinite delay in the negotiations.[21]

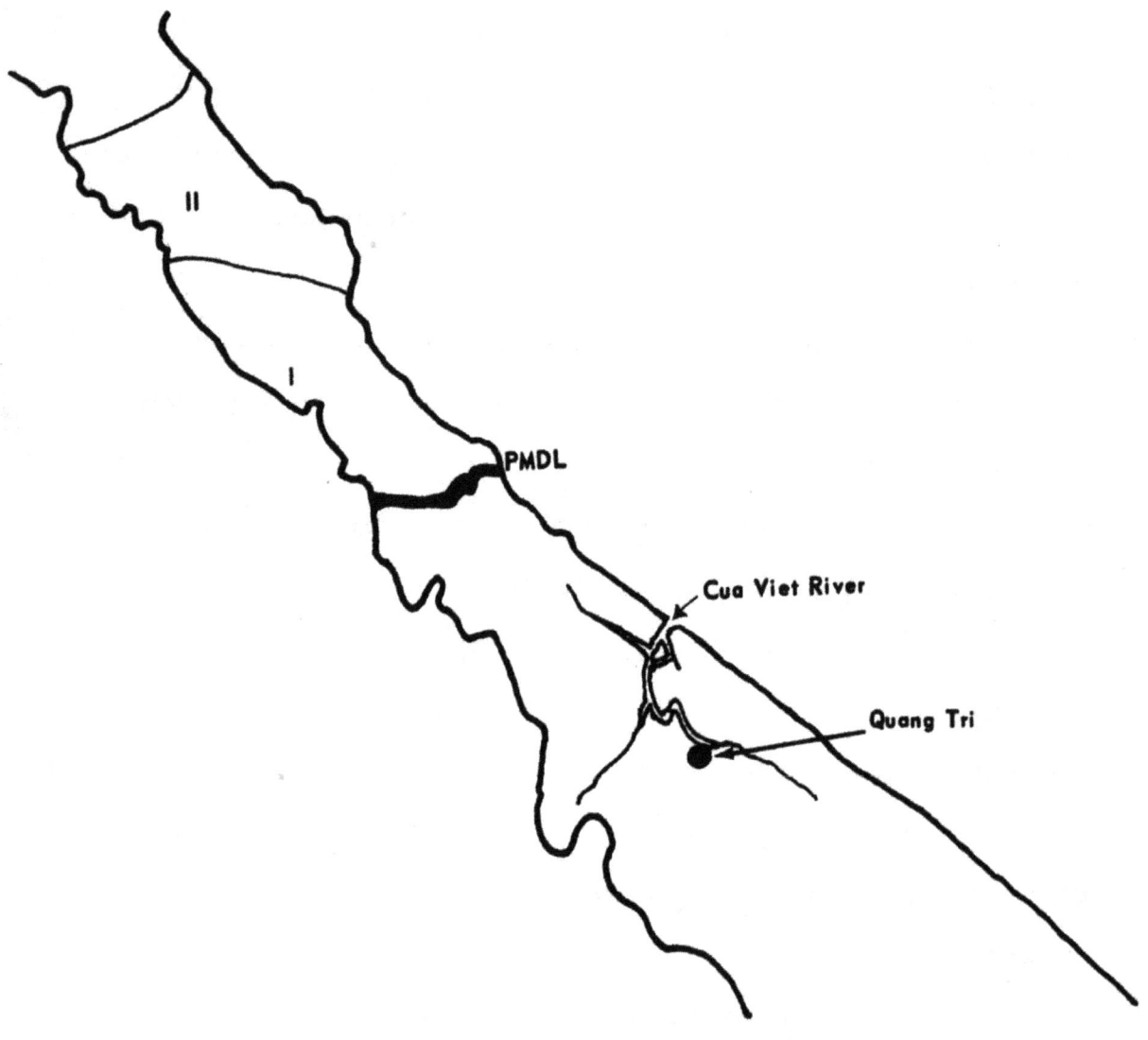

**DMZ and Cua Viet River**

**FIGURE 5**

The renewed bombing north of the 20th parallel, designed to encourage more serious discussions of peace, was attributed by the Nixon Administration to have directly brought about the peace agreement signed on 27 January 1973. The period prior to and after the signing of the agreement was marked by many changes in the ROE for the RVN. The most important was the cessation of all acts of force by U.S. forces in the RVN. This was promulgated by the JCS on 24 January 1973.[22]

On 27 January, the JCS defined the level at which U.S. air could be used after the cease-fire became effective on 28 January 1973. Since all acts of force initiated by U.S. forces had been stopped, the new ROE were mainly concerned with the protection of U.S. forces until their complete withdrawal could be accomplished by 28 March 1973. The new rules concerned all air operations in the RVN, specifically, emergency recovery bases, SAR operations, and other activities related to U.S. air power in the RVN. The operating authorities which affected the RVN, promulgated by the JCS and made effective with the cease-fire, are shown in Table 1, which follows.

(TS) This series of changes basically ended the role of the ROE in the RVN. Other changes of the ROE made prior to the total cease-fire for U.S. forces in SEA in August 1973 were mainly concerned with operations in Laos and Cambodia. The changes, as they occurred, are discussed in appropriate chapters which follow.*

TABLE 1

SEASIA OPERATING AUTHORITIES --
CEASE-FIRE IN RVN AND NVN (U)[23]

RVN

1. Operations using TACAIR, B-52s, rotary wing gunships, artillery, naval bombardment, other fire, or ordnance expenditures are authorized against hostile forces in South Vietnam only when in direct support of U.S. personnel under enemy attack. This authority expires at completion of withdrawal.

2. Immediate pursuit: After completion of withdrawal when U.S. forces are attacked, U.S. forces may, if required for self-defense, conduct immediate pursuit of attacking forces into RVN territorial seas or airspace.

---

* (U) A complete recapitulation of the ROE which became effective on 28 January 1973 is provided in Appendix A.

a. Immediate pursuit into RVN territorial seas or airspace must be continuous and uninterrupted and is authorized to protect U.S. forces and only until the hostile aircraft or vessels no longer pose an immediate threat to U.S. forces. Immediate pursuit shall not include prolonged pursuit deep into RVN airspace.

b. U.S. forces in immediate pursuit are authorized to attack other forces or installations encountered only when attacked first by them, then only to the extent necessary for self-defense.

3. Defensive response: Defensive responses within the RVN are authorized only to protect U.S. forces and only when all other alternatives have failed. Defensive response may be made only after actual hostile fire has been encountered and must be limited to an immediate response against only those forces actually firing at U.S. forces.

4. U.S. aircraft are authorized to overfly RVN as necessary for the conduct of approved operations in SE Asia.

5. Air reconnaissance operations (manned or unmanned) are authorized throughout RVN as required.

6. Surveillance activities, similar to Market Time (coastal surveillance of RVN by USN), may be conducted in and over the territorial waters of RVN and international waters of the South China Sea to provide early warning to the Republic of Vietnam Armed Forces (RVNAF); however, surveillance operations in RVN territorial waters and airspace will be authorized following U.S. withdrawal only when appropriately cleared by the Government of Vietnam (GVN).

7. After completion of withdrawal, RVN airbases may be used as emergency recovery bases for U.S. military aircraft conducting approved operations in SEA. RVN airbases may be designated as weather alternates only for flights terminating in RVN, or when approved by the GVN.

8. Deleted.

9. U.S. forces (air, ground, and naval) may provide armed escort for U.S. forces movements within the RVN during withdrawal.

10. Deleted.

11. Air and surface logistics operations related to replenishment of consumable supplies (POL, ammo, spare parts, etc.) and maintenance support, are authorized within the terms of the cease-fire agreement.

12. SAR operations may be conducted for U.S. personnel throughout RVN. During the conduct of such operations, munitions expenditure, including RCA (CS), may be used only under the terms of the defensive response provisions. In addition, when determined by COMUSMACV/U.S. Support Activities Group/7AF (USSAG/7AF) that such action is necessary, ground security forces may be used in SAR efforts in the RVN. During the period of withdrawal, SAR operations are authorized for friendly aircrews in emergency situations beyond RVNAF capability.

13. Recovery of U.S. aircraft is authorized.

14. Attacks:

a. In the event of a minor attack (as defined in the basic ROE for SEA) against U.S. forces, the on-scene commander is authorized the use of full internal firepower (small arms, automatic weapons, mortars, artillery, and rotary-wing gunships) under his command and/or operational control to repulse the attack and insure the safety of his forces.

b. In the event of a major attack (as defined in basic ROE for SEA) against U.S. forces, the on-scene commander is authorized the use of full integrated firepower, internal firepower, TACAIR and naval gunfire ships (NGFS) necessary to repulse the attack and insure the safety of U.S. forces.

    c. Commanders will immediately report any attack on U.S./friendly forces and seek guidance from higher authority. Reports will include the extent of the attack, reaction, assessment of the situation, and other pertinent information.

    d. No hostile actions or counter-attacks, other than for direct self-defense, are authorized without approval from higher authority.

15. U.S. forces may be used in response to requests for evacuation assistance in the RVN for the following categories of individuals and equipment: U.S. military personnel, U.S. nationals or certain employees of the United States and friendly personnel as may be directed by the CJCS and such sensitive equipment as may be designated by the CJCS. U.S. forces may be used ashore as deemed necessary by the on-scene commander to insure security of evacuation operations.

16. U.S. forces based on or operating from bases in the Republic of Vietnam will <u>not</u> be employed in support

of operations in Laos or Cambodia.

17. During withdrawal from the RVN, U.S. forces are authorized to conduct normal training to maintain unit readiness. No ordnance other than that normally regarded as self-defensive in nature (AIM-7, AIM-9, 20mm) will be carried aboard U.S. aircraft conducting training missions in the vicinity of RVN and NVN. No naval gunfire will be initiated in the cease-fire area or against NVN ships or watercraft of any type except in accordance with the provisions of defensive response outlined in paragraph 5 above.

18. RVN positive control area (PCA). The RVN PCA is that area of Laos and Cambodia within 10 nautical miles of the RVN border extending from 16 degrees 40 minutes north latitude southward to the Gulf of Thailand. All air strikes in the RVN PCA will be conducted under the control of a FAG except for B-52 strikes conducted using all-weather bombing systems. Air strikes in the RVN PCA will be planned and conducted in a manner so as to preclude the impact of ordnance in the RVN.*

---

* (U) The ROE concerning Joint Casualty Resolution Center (JCRC) operations have been omitted in this and subsequent tables. For information on this topic, consult the CHECO report, <u>Joint Personnel Recovery in Southeast Asia</u>.

## CHAPTER III

## NORTH VIETNAM

(S) With the initiation of the interdiction campaign in NVN in May 1972 (Linebacker), the restrictions of the ROE were made to apply primarily to the areas around Hanoi and Haiphong, to third country shipping, and to the PRC buffer zone. Although the 20-nautical-mile PRC buffer zone itself remained unchanged in alignment, CINCPAC somewhat relaxed the restrictions which applied to the zone on 11 October 1972.[24] This loosening of constraints allowed strike and support forces to enter the PRC buffer zone restricted area when conducting or supporting JCS/CINCPAC-approved strikes in the buffer zone or when engaged (or in support of) the immediate pursuit of enemy aircraft.[25]

(U) As the interdiction bombing continued in North Vietnam, it gradually became evident that Hanoi was being convinced of the necessity for more serious negotiations in concluding a cease-fire. As matters developed during September and October, so much progress was made on a draft agreement that the United States was rather taken aback when the North Vietnamese insisted that the agreement be completed and signed by 31 October 1972.[26]

(S) This sudden change by the North Vietnamese toward negotiating a peace in Vietnam again prompted U.S. authorities to order the cessation of all U.S. air operations north of 20 degrees north latitude in NVN. The only operations authorized in North Vietnam, beginning at 0700 hours on 23 October, were those of Giant Scale* and photo drones.[27] This suspension of bombing in the north was intended to convey to the North Vietnamese the seriousness of U.S. intentions and to signal to all the progress that was being made at the negotiating table in Paris.[28]

(U) While Hanoi insisted that the draft agreement be signed by 31 October -- in a complete reversal of its policy over the previous three years of refusing to carry on meaningful negotiations -- the United States refrained from doing so for a number of reasons. It was thought that a delay was necessary because there had been mounting evidence that the Communists were planning

---

*(U) Giant Scale--Reconnaissance conducted by SAC SR-71s in SEA.

to take advantage of the cease-fire by suddenly launching a military offensive; because Hanoi had made public comments on the possibility of a coalition government in South Vietnam in direct contradiction to the firm agreement that such was not envisioned in the settlement; and because the RVN had opposed some of the changes, indicating the need for more time to consider the proposals.[29]

(TS) In essence, the ROE were again structured in a form similar to that which existed prior to the resumption of the bombing of North Vietnam in May 1972. Specifically, no operations were authorized north of the 20th parallel. The immediate pursuit of enemy aircraft into NVN was authorized, but only as far north as 20 degrees 30 minutes north latitude. Protective reaction strikes were not authorized against AAA/SAM or coastal defense sites or their integral radars which were located north of 20 degrees north latitude and which fired at or were activated against U.S. or friendly aircraft. The only action allowed in the event of enemy mine countermeasures activity was the immediate notification of the CJCS.[30] The rationale for these extremely restrictive measures was conveyed by the JCS on 4 November, quoting guidance from the Secretary of Defense (SecDef);

> (TS) In imposing these operating limitations, SecDef noted that the restrictions reflect the basic guidance that air-to-surface and surface-to-surface ordnance will not impact in North Vietnam north of the 20th parallel and further that hot pursuit is authorized in North Vietnam only up to 20 degrees 30 minutes north latitude. Accordingly, request that you take steps to insure that the spirit and intent of the current operating authorities as they relate to North Vietnam are clearly understood and diligently followed by all personnel in SEA. While limiting the tactical flexibility of US forces operating in the vicinity of the northern part of NVN, adherence to these latest restrictions is critical to on going sensitive political negotiations.[31]

(U) As the substantiveness of the Paris negotiations fluctuated so did the restrictions on the use of air power in NVN. The attempts to influence negotiations with military power were reflected in the changes of the ROE promulgated by the JCS.

(TS) On 2 November 1972, B-52 strikes were restricted to military targets in NVN to a northernmost limit of 18 degrees 45 minutes north latitude.[32] This restriction was relaxed somewhat when COMUSMACV declared his intention to order B-52 strikes up to 19 degrees 15 minutes north to counter a North Vietnamese logistics campaign. CINCPAC's concurrence and strong recommendation resulted in the JCS authorization of bombing up to 19 degrees 15 minutes north on 5 November.[33]

(U) These custodial restrictions on the use of air power, including the total bombing halt above the 20th parallel, continued through November and into December. It was in the middle of December, President Nixon recounted, when the next change in national direction became necessary. The peace negotiations had gone well in November. However, when the talks were resumed on 4 December after a nine-day recess, a noticeable change had taken place in North Vietnamese attitudes. They began the new round of peace negotiations by withdrawing all the changes which had been accepted in November and injecting new issues whenever current ones neared solution. It became clear that the North Vietnamese had no intention of agreeing on a settlement; a total impasse between the parties occurred.

Another recess began on 13 December 1972. It was evident to U.S. negotiators that Hanoi was stalling for time and strong measures were required.[34] Moreover, the South Vietnamese were still skeptical of certain proposals.

This deadlock in negotiations prompted U.S. strategists to abolish nearly all restraints on the use of tactical air power over North Vietnam. The execution order for the resumption of bombing north of the 20th parallel came on 17 December 1972 and became effective at noon of the 18th.[35] The bombing campaign was given the code name Linebacker II (LB-II) and lasted for 12 days. Initially, LB-II was to be a three-day, maximum effort operation in the Hanoi/Haiphong area. On 19 December, however, the JCS directed that the operation be continued until further notice.[36]

The objective of LB-II was the maximum destruction of selected military targets in and around the Hanoi/Haiphong complex and the buffer zone. Airfields and SAM sites could be struck as the situation dictated.[37] Of particular importance was the destruction of power plants. The second objective of the

LB-II operation was to isolate Hanoi by the destruction of targets which connected -- electrically and logistically -- Hanoi with the rest of North Vietnam. This was to be attained by the destruction of the northeast LOC (first priority) and the northwest LOC (second priority). The interdiction of these LOCs included strikes against railroad bridges, yards and shops, and highway bridges, and the mining of waterways.[38]

(S) When it became evident to the highest Washington authorities that the North Vietnamese were again ready to resume serious negotiations, the bombing above the 20th parallel was halted. This occurred on 30 December, 12 days after the initiation of LB-II.[39] At the same time, all military operations above 20 degrees north latitude in NVN and adjacent waters were terminated. SAR operations which were currently in effect could be concluded. Air and naval operations south of 20 degrees north latitude were to continue under the existing ROE which remained the same as they had been prior to the start of LB-II.[40]

(U) The impact of the bombing north of the 20th parallel undoubtedly caused the North Vietnamese to reconsider the peace proposals. The beginning of January 1973, the days immediately following the Linebacker operation, saw rapid progress on the remaining issues of the peace agreement. The South Vietnamese agreed to some of the changes on which they had had reservations and changed their position on other questions for the sake of concluding the settlement.[41]

With serious negotiations well underway and the final drafting of an agreement nearly completed, the JCS suspended all offensive operations against NVN effective at 1500Z (2200 hours local time) on 15 January 1973.[42] The new rules prohibited any offensive operations (air strikes, artillery fire, naval bombardment, mining/seeding, and other fire or munitions expenditure) in NVN including the DMZ north of the provisional military demarcation line (PMDL) and within the 12-nautical-mile territorial waters of NVN. Overflights of NVN and the DMZ north of the PMDL in connection with operations in the RVN, Laos, and Cambodia, including psychological operations were prohibited. Immediate pursuit was authorized into NVN territorial seas or airspace in reaction to hostile acts against U.S./allied forces operating outside NVN territorial seas or airspace, but was limited only to the NVN element initiating the hostile action. Reconnaissance was limited to drones and SR-71 aircraft and the limitations already placed on these operations remained in effect (drones were prohibited from operating in the PRC buffer zone and SR-71 aircraft were not allowed to approach closer than ten nautical miles of the PRC border).[43]

(C) In order to follow the JCS guidance in avoiding overflight of NVN, Seventh Air Force implemented the positive control area,* positive control zone,** and the NVN border warning procedures*** on 16 January 1973.[44]

(U) On 23 January the final meeting at Paris

---

*(S-XCL-3) The positive control area was that area of Laos within 10 nautical miles of the NVN/RVN border between 19 degrees 00 minutes north and 16 degrees 40 minutes north. This was defined in 7AF OPORD 71-17, Ch 4, 19 Jun 72, p. IV-3. (CMR S-729, 104)
**(S-XCL-3) The positive control zone was that area of RVN between 16 degrees 40 minutes north and the southern boundary of the DMZ. This zone was defined in 7AF OPORD 71-17, Ch 4, 19 Jun 72, p. II-2. (CMR S-729, 098)
***(S XGDS-3) The border warning procedures were used to prevent inadvertent entry into restricted airspace. These were explained in 7AF Manual 55-1, "TACAIR Operational Procedures," 15 May 74, p. 9-2. (CMR S-986, 179).

took place. The United States and North Vietnam, with the concurrence of their allies, initialed the peace agreement. The official signing of the agreement occurred on 27 January 1973. The internationally supervised cease-fire throughout Vietnam became effective at 0700 Eastern Standard Time, Saturday, 27 January.[45]

The operating authorities which affected operations in NVN at the time of the cease-fire were as follows:

TABLE 2

SEASIA OPERATING AUTHORITIES -- CEASE-FIRE
IN RVN AND NVN (U)[45a]

<u>NVN</u>

1. Military operations of all types are prohibited in NVN territory and territorial airspace/seas except:

    a. U.S. forces are authorized to operate in NVN territory, internal waters, and territorial airspace/seas for mine countermeasures operations, logistical support and the like as promulgated by separate directive.

    b. Search and rescue operations may be conducted

for U.S. personnel throughout NVN. During the conduct of such operations, munitions expenditures, including RCA (CS), must be conducted only under the terms of defensive response (see para 1d).

c. Immediate pursuit: When U.S. forces are under attack, U.S. forces may, if required for self-defense, conduct immediate pursuit of attacking forces into NVN territorial waters or airspace.

(1) Immediate pursuit into NVN territorial waters or airspace must be continuous and uninterrupted and is authorized to protect U.S. forces and only until the hostile aircraft or vessels no longer pose an immediate threat to U.S. forces. Immediate pursuit shall not include prolonged pursuit deep into hostile airspace.

(2) U.S. forces in immediate pursuit are authorized to attack other forces or installations encountered, only when attacked first by them, then only to the extent necessary for self-defense.

d. Defensive response: In the event U.S. forces are fired upon by forces located in NVN, every effort will be made to withdraw. Defensive responses into

NVN are authorized to protect U.S. forces only when all other alternatives have failed. Defensive response may be made only after actual hostile fire has been encountered and must be limited to an immediate response against only those forces actually firing at U.S. forces. Defensive reponse will not be initiated based only upon activation of NVN radars.

CHAPTER IV

## LAOS

(S) The air war in Laos was superintended in much the same way it was in NVN, influenced as strategists were by both North Vietnamese tactics and political jousting. The U.S. experience in Laos through September 1972 had shown that ground combat activity, both enemy and friendly, and supporting friendly air operations were at the mercy of seasonal weather changes. Most activity occurred during the dry season when North Vietnamese transported the major portion of their men and supplies through the eastern part of Laos. Activity during the wet season was restricted mainly to preparing for the next dry season. This involved the stockpiling of material and improving and expanding their infiltration routes.[46] After September 1972, the peace negotiations (initiated on 18 September 1972) between the Laotian parties also contributed to the changes which occurred in the application of air power in Laos.[47]

(S) Except for the ROE changes which accompanied the Laotian and NVN peace negotiations, the majority of changes affected the special operating areas (SOA) and Raven control boxes. These changes were in the nature of validating or deleting specific SOAs or parts thereof, in allowing special armed reconnaissance along certain routes and route segments, of FAC authorization for conducting air strikes, and for the expansion or contraction of the SOAs and Raven control boxes.

In October 1972, when the progress of peace negotiations brought optimism for a cease-fire in RVN and NVN, the JCS promulgated a series of SEA operating authorities which affected air operations in Laos. Changes were made in the approval/validation authority as well as specific modifications in the use of air power. Tactical air (TACAIR) strikes, including the use of fixed wing gunships, could be conducted throughout Laos under the overall approval of the American Embassy (AmEmb) Vientiane. Strikes in Barrel Roll (BR) North, against Sam Neua, within the BR East buffer zone, and within five kilometers of known or suspected Chinese positions in BR East and BR West required JCS approval and coordination with the Assistant Secretary of Defense (ASD). Airstrikes and armed reconnaissance could be conducted within the BR East buffer zone under the following guidelines:[48]

(1) In an area bounded by the UTM* coordinates UGXX80 on the north, 19 degrees north latitude on the south, the ten nautical mile buffer zone boundary line on the west, and a line four nautical miles west of the border of NVN on the east.

(2) Within 200 meters of Route 7, up to two kilometers west of the NVN border.

(3) Within 200 meters of Route 72 (Route 7 bypass), up to a point two kilometers west of the NVN border.

(4) When requested by the AmEmb Vientiane in support of friendly sites under enemy attack, Arc Light strikes required the approval of CINCPAC and CINCSAC acting jointly and in coordination with the AmEmb when they were to be carried out against targets in Steel Tiger.

Arc Light strikes in BR had to be requested 24 hours in advance in order to allow time for an

---

* Universal Transverse Mercator map projection

appropriate JCS review and approval. FAC operations in BR East or BR West required JCS approval in coordination with ASD.[48a] These operating authorities were initially effective through 1 December 1972, but were extended through 31 December by the JCS.[49]

(C) The sensitivity of the negotiations with the North Vietnamese was reflected in the tightening of the ROE for Laos, particularly in the changes along the buffer zone adjacent to the NVN border. On 1 November 1972, Seventh Air Force prohibited U.S. air strikes within the buffer zone unless targets were specifically validated by the AmEmb/Office of the U.S. Air Attache (OUSAIRA), Vientiane and approved by Seventh Air Force. Extreme caution was to be taken to prevent the inadvertent penetration of the NVN border.[50]

(C/NOFORN) During the rest of November, the ROE changes again affected the validation of the SOAs, Raven control boxes, and the use of armed reconnaissance. On 3 November, a segment of Route 4/7 from the western boundary of SOA-2 to the Nam Chat Ford, within 200 meters on either side of the route, was validated for armed reconnaissance by gunships and escorts.[51] This was followed closely by a revision of SOA-2 and the Raven control area south in BR West.[52] On 15 November 1972, the AmEmb Vientiane validated the Saravane town area in MR IV for strikes by U.S. TACAIR under the control of a validated FAG. This change opened up only the immediate environs of the town proper.[53] Validation of visual armed reconnaissance within 200 meters of Route 23, including its spurs and bypasses from a point just west of Paksong (XB290780) to Lao Ngam (XB083775), occurred on 27 November. The expanded strike authority allowed strikes against tanks, trucks, and other military vehicles using the route. Gunships could FAC for escort and other strike aircraft. Strikes against moving military vehicles west of Lao Ngam on Route 23 could be conducted only if the gunship was under the control of validated MR IV FAC. Also included in the 27 November change was validation for armed reconnaissance along Route 23 from Thateng (XC486050) south to a point east of Paksong (XB360797) and was subject to the following rules:

(1) No strikes could be conducted by U.S. aircraft closer than 500 meters to the nearest structure

associated with the four active villages along the validated segment of the route.

(2) Strikes could be conducted by gunships throughout an area extending out to 200 meters on either side of the road, its spurs, and immediate bypasses.

(3) Gunships could also control fast mover escorts subject to the same restrictions.

(C) The armed reconnaissance, the 200 meter restriction, and FAC duties for gunships were also authorized along Route 161, including its spurs and bypasses from coordinates XC101118 to XC151099.[54]

(C) Following a recommendation by the AmEmb Vientiane on 13 December 1972, Seventh Air Force, on 14 December, restricted gunships, using beacon-tracking sensors in support of troops in contact (TIC), from firing closer than 200 meters of friendly positions during instrument meteorological conditions. In addition, strikes closer than 500 meters to occupied villages could not be conducted without the approval of the appropriate AmEmb-designated authority (Smokey Control/Painter Control) who would reserve judgment until apprised of the situation -- being assured that the gunship was in radio contact with an authorized FAG, and that both ground and airborne equipment were functional. The change affected only the validation of targets associated with direct troop support.[55]

(C/NOFORN) On 19 December, the AmEmb Vientiane issued a no bomb line to preclude inadvertent air strikes against exposed troop positions because of the insertion of air intelligence teams along the SL East/West boundary in MR III. This restriction applied only to U.S. aircraft and was effective through 26 December.[56]

(C) Christmas Day brought two changes for the ROE. The first was the establishment of a ten nautical mile prohibited area around the city of Luang Prabang in northern Laos.[57] The other, affecting southern Laos, established a new armed reconnaissance area extending in two directions from Thateng. It extended south along Route 23 for five kilometers and for 200 meters on either side of the road; it also extended east along Route 16 to Ban Phone and for 200 meters on either side of the road.[58]

(C/NOFORN) An increase in the operating area in and adjacent to the Plaine des Jarres was approved by the AmEmb Vientiane on 27 December, expanding SOA-2 and redefining Raven control area north and Raven control area south.[59] The AmEmb Vientiane also redefined the beacon delivery zone (BDZ) which overlapped portions of both Raven control area south and SOA-2. The original BDZ had been established on 13 November to assist in the employment of F-111 assets in BR.[60] This BDZ was redesignated BDZ South and a second BDZ, BDZ North, was established around Bouam Long to facilitate strikes in the defense of this Royal Laotian Government (RLG) enclave. F-111 strikes were authorized, using the J-band beacon,* at a distance of 1,000 meters or more from friendly positions. The ROE for strikes in SOA-2 stipulated that any approved IFR (instrument flight rules) strike system could be used, day or night, without FAC control. This included F-111, radar, and J-band beacon systems.[61] The AmEmb Vientiane again redefined

---

* (U) The J-band beacon was a system used by the F-111 to determine an exact reference point on the ground.

the boundaries of the northern BDZ on 31 December and the boundaries of the southern BDZ on 4 January 1973. However, the ROE for the BDZs and SOA-2 otherwise remained unchanged.[62]

(C) Although the U.S. Embassy in Vientiane again redefined SOA-2, modified the Raven control area south, and validated certain segments of Route 4/7 during the last of December 1972 and the first part of January 1973; there were no associated ROE changes until 8 January when armed reconnaissance was authorized within 200 meters of Route 4/7 from the junction of Routes 13 and 4/7, east through Muong Soui to SOA-2. The validation included all immediate trails, junctions, and bypasses. Gunships had to be in contact with an authorized ground FAG outside these areas and all active friendly villages and structures were to be avoided by 500 meters.[63]

(C) The reduction of offensive operations in NVN also resulted in the restriction of certain activities in Laos. Most affected were the U.S. activities in BR East along the NVN buffer zone. On 18 January, three days after the suspension of all offensive operations against NVN, Seventh Air Force prohibited air strikes in the buffer zone unless the targets were specifically validated by the AmEmb Vientiane and approved by CINCPAC and the JCS.[64]

(TS) With the advent of the cease-fire in both Vietnams, a new set of operating authorities were issued by the JCS. The section affecting Laos is outlined in the following table:

TABLE 3

(TS) SEASIA OPERATING AUTHORITIES --
CEASE-FIRE IN RVN AND NVN (U)[65]

<u>LAOS</u>

1. TACAIR, Arc Light, and fixed wing gunship strikes may be conducted in support of the RLG, however, it is mandatory that air operations in Laos are conducted in such a manner that there will be no cause to overfly NVN territory or deliver ordnance against targets in NVN.

2. Operating Areas. Laos is divided as defined in 7AF OPORD 71-17.

3. Search and Rescue:

(A) SAR operations for U.S. personnel may be conducted throughout Laos.

(B) In emergency situations beyond the capabilities of Allied Air Forces and as approved by COMUSMACV/USSAG/7AF on a case-by-case basis, SAR operations may be conducted for Allied aircrews in Laos.

(C) During the conduct of SAR operations when necessary to protect the SAR forces and insure safe recovery of personnel:

    (1) Ground fire may be returned.

    (2) RCA (may be used).

    (3) On a case-by-case basis, when determined by COMUSMACV/USSAG/7AF that such action is necessary, ground security forces may be used in SAR efforts throughout Laos for U.S. personnel.

4. Recovery of U.S. aircraft is authorized in low risk areas throughout Laos.

5. Reconnaissance:

(A) Reconnaissance aircraft are authorized to operate in Laos with armed escort and flak suppression as required except as specified below:

    (1) Manned tactical reconnaissance aircraft, to include armed escort and other reconnaissance support, are not authorized in Barrel Roll North or

within five kilometers of known or suspected Chinese positions in Barrel Roll East and Barrel Roll West unless approved by the JCS.

    (2) High and low photo drones over Laos will not approach closer than 25 nautical miles to the PRC border.

    (3) SR-71 and U-2 flight tracks over Laos will not approach closer than 10 nautical miles to the PRC border.

    (4) Manned airborne SIGINT (signal intelligence) collection aircraft other than SR-71 and U-2 operating over Laos will not approach closer than 25 nautical miles to the PRC border.

6. Passive Aerial Operations: Inflight refueling, airborne early warning, command and control, electronic warfare, radio relay and the like, are authorized in support of approved combat air operations.

7. TACAIR, Arc Light, and fixed wing gunship strikes may be conducted throughout Laos under the overall approval of AmEmb Vientiane in support of the RLG.

    (A) Strikes in Barrel Roll North, strikes against Sam Neua, and strikes within five kilometers of known or suspected Chinese positions located in Barrel Roll

East and Barrel Roll West require JCS approval.

(B) Arc Light strikes may be conducted against targets in Laos as approved by COMUSMACV/USSAG/7AF.

8. FAC Operations. U.S. forward air controllers may control U.S., Lao, or third country airstrikes in Laos subject to the same limitations imposed on U.S. tactical air activity in Laos.

9. Attache/Deputy Chief Activities. U.S. military personnel assigned to DEPCHJUSMAGTHAI and the U.S. Embassy in Vientiane may participate in the following combat related functions:

(A) Training of Lao pilots to include delivery of ordnance against live targets in Laos and,

(B) Flying on RLAF AC-47s in an observer status.

10. In coordination with AmEmb Vientiane, U.S. helicopters may be employed in support of operations in Laos as follows:

(A) Routine day-to-day operations are authorized to include MedEvac, resupply within capabilities, positioning of various teams and replacements, deployment of battalion-sized forces, evacuation of refugees and flood relief, salvage, psychological operations, lift for artillery, construction equipment and inoperative aircraft.

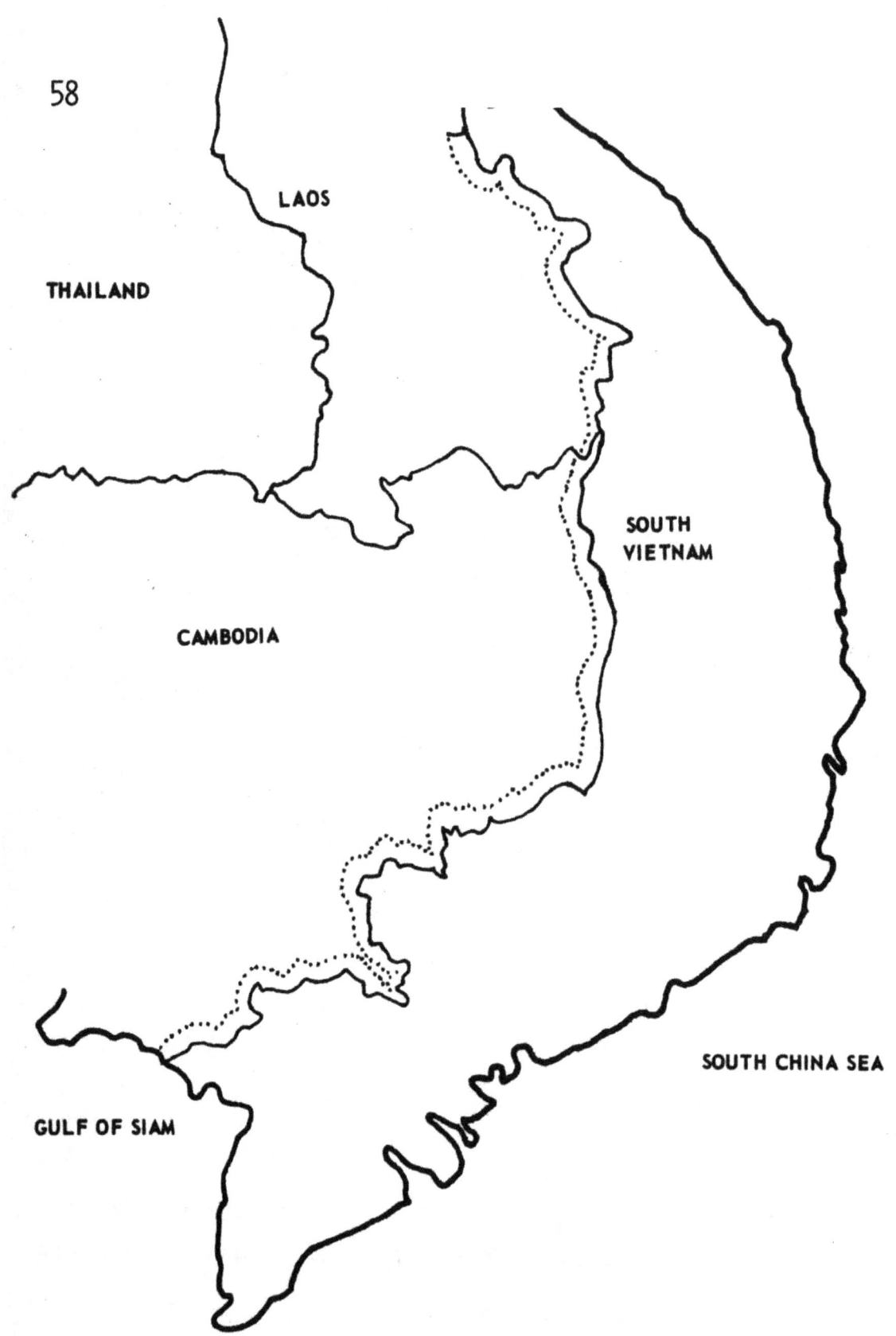

(B) JCS approval is required for any operation which is politically sensitive because of its size, scope, location, timing or duration or which poses a substantial risk to U.S. assets. Support of multi-battalion operations requires JCS approval.

11. U.S. forces are authorized to conduct psychological operations (PSYOP) against enemy controlled and contested areas of Laos and the Laotian trail system used by NVA. Printed media, gift packages, loudspeakers and use of U.S. aircraft and crews for dissemination of materials are authorized.

\*     \*     \*     \*     \*

(U) The ROE which applied to air operations in Southeast Asia after the cease-fire in the RVN and NVN are listed in Appendix A.

(S/NOFORN) The cease-fire in the RVN and NVN also altered the control of operations in the Laos PCA. Effective 28 January 1973, the ten nautical-mile-wide PCA in Laos was extended south, from 16 degrees 40 minutes north, continuously along the Laos/RVN border and the Khmer/RVN border, to the Gulf of Thailand. Refer to Figure 6. FAC aircraft could operate in the PCA when fragged, but were required to take every feasible precaution to prevent the penetration of the RVN border. TACAIR could only operate in the PCA under FAC control.[66] The FAC and strike aircraft procedures that applied to the RVN border and PCA south of 16 degrees 40 minutes north latitude were:

(1) Aircrews could not enter Steel Tiger without first establishing positive communications with the primary control agency.

(2) Guard frequency had to be monitored at all times for MIG/border warnings.

(3) IFF/SIF had to be operational on all FAC aircraft and on at least one aircraft in the strike flight.

(4) FACs had to establish radio contact with the primary control agency upon entering the assigned operational area.

(5) FACs could conduct strikes only when the target was positively identified and the attack could be made without overflying NVN. They also were required to keep the strike flight advised of their relative position to the border.

(6) Aircrews could not deliver ordnance on

headings toward the NVN border unless the bomb run was preplanned to allow a turn after bomb release to insure border clearance. When targets in close proximity to the NVN border were scheduled, special instructions would be issued in the frag order for the mission. Aircrews and FACs were jointly responsible for preventing penetration of NVN airspace.[67]

(C) The remainder of January saw only a few changes, those dealing with the validation of segments of Routes 4/7 and 16/23. Basically, the ROE associated with the use of armed reconnaissance along the validated routes remained the same.[68]

(C) On 3 February, in order to permit the bombing of military targets in defense of Thakhek without further validation, SOA-8 was established southeast of Thakhek. In SOA-8, strikes were approved without FAC control but only when in VFR (visual flight rules) conditions. All ordnance approved for use in Laos, including napalm, was authorized. (Only by the specific approval of the AmEmb Vientiane could area denial munitions be used.) All active villages and associated active structures had to be avoided by 500 meters.[69] Because of the fluid ground situation, the movement of friendly positions, and the establishment of two no bomb lines, the ROE applicable to SOA-8 were changed on 15 February to preclude the use of TACAIR strikes unless they were under FAC control. The FAC controlling TACAIR strikes was required to be in contact with the appropriate ground commander.[70]

On 21 February 1973, the peace settlement which had been under negotiation by the Laotian parties was concluded, becoming effective at 220500Z February 1973. Because of this settlement, the JCS distributed an entirely new set of operating authorities for Laos (refer to Table 4 which follows) and redefined the Southeast Asia Basic ROE (refer to Appendix B). The new operating authorities were:

TABLE 4

OPERATING AUTHORITIES -- LAOS (U)[71]

A. Operating Areas: Laos is divided into Barrel Roll and Steel Tiger, as defined by a line from UF8927 to WF1140. It is further divided into five operating areas identified as BR North, BR East, BR West, SL East, and SL West. (The boundaries of these operating areas are defined in 7AF OPORD 71-17.)

B. U.S. aircraft are authorized to overfly Laos if necessary for the conduct of approved operations in SEA. However, utmost caution must be exercised to insure that there will be no cause to overfly NVN territory or deliver ordnance against targets in NVN.

C. Immediate Pursuit: When under attack, U.S. forces may, if required for self-defense, conduct immediate pursuit of attacking forces into Laotian airspace.

1. Immediate pursuit into Laotian airspace must be continuous and uninterrupted and is authorized to protect U.S. forces and only until the hostile aircraft no longer pose an immediate threat to U.S. forces. Immediate pursuit shall not include prolonged pursuit deep into Laotian airspace.

2. U.S. forces in immediate pursuit are authorized to attack other forces or installations encountered only when attacked first by them, then only to the extent necessary for self-defense.

D. Defensive Response: Defensive responses within Laos are authorized to protect U.S. forces only when all other alternatives have failed. Defensive response may be made only after actual hostile fire has been encountered and must be limited to an immediate response against only those forces actually firing at U.S. forces.

E. Air reconnaissance (manned and unmanned) and SIGINT operations are authorized throughout Laos, except as specified below:

1. Manned tactical reconnaissance aircraft are not authorized to penetrate the NVN border, overfly Barrel Roll North, or to fly within five kilometers of known or suspected Chinese positions in Barrel Roll East or Barrel Roll West, unless approved by the JCS.

2. High and low photo drones will not penetrate the NVN border nor approach closer than 25 nautical miles to the PRC border.

3. SR-71 and U-2 reconnaissance missions will not overfly the NVN border nor approach closer than 10 nautical miles to the PRC border.

4. Manned airborne SIGINT collection aircraft (other than SR-71 and U-2) operating over Laos will not penetrate the NVN border nor approach closer than 25 nautical miles to the PRC border.

F. Omitted

G. Recovery of U.S. aircraft is authorized as required throughout Laos.

H. SAR operations may be conducted for U.S. personnel throughout Laos, during the conduct of such operations, munitions expenditures including RCA (CS) may be used under the terms of the defensive response provisions. SAR operations may be conducted in support of friendly aircrews in emergency situations when beyond RLAF capability.

1. Air and surface logistics replenishment operations are authorized in accordance with terms provided separately.

2. Nothing in these authorities shall be construed as precluding a commander from using all means at his disposal to exercise inherent right and responsibility to conduct operations for self-defense of his forces.

\*       \*       \*       \*       \*

(C) On 6 March 1973, a Laos border restricted area was established which prevented U.S. aircraft from penetrating closer than five nautical miles to the

Laotian border from any nearby country. Aircraft on published or radar approaches to and departures from Nakhon Phanom RTAFB, Thailand, and operations specifically approved by the U.S. Support Activities Group (USSAG/7AF) were the only exceptions to this restriction.[72]

On 31 March, the JCS again redefined the operating authorities for Laos. These new authorities (refer to Table 5 below) superseded all previous authorities and became effective on 291600Z March 1973:[73]

TABLE 5

SEASIA OPERATING AUTHORITIES--LAOS (U)

1. Operating Areas: Laos is divided as defined in 7AF OPORD 71-17.
2. U.S. aircraft are authorized to overfly Laos as necessary for the conduct of approved operations in SE Asia. However, utmost caution must be exercised to insure that there will be no cause to overfly NVN territory or deliver ordnance against targets in NVN.
3. Upon request by the Royal Lao Government (RLG) and the AmEmb Vientiane, you are authorized to engage and

destroy NVN MIG aircraft conducting operations in Laos. In operations under this authority, U.S. aircraft may not conduct immediate pursuit of NVN aircraft into NVN airspace unless the immediate pursuit requirements are fulfilled. (I.e., when U.S. forces are under attack, U.S. forces may, if required for self-defense, conduct immediate pursuit of attacking forces into NVN territorial waters or airspace. Immediate pursuit into NVN territorial waters or airspace must be continuous and uninterrupted and is authorized for the protection of U.S. forces and only until the hostile aircraft or vessels no longer pose an immediate threat to U.S. forces. Immediate pursuit shall not include prolonged pursuit deep into hostile airspace. U.S. forces in immediate pursuit are authorized to attack other forces or installations encountered only when attacked first by them, and then only to the extent necessary for self-defense.)

4. Defensive Response: Except as outlined in paragraph 3 above, defensive responses within Laos are authorized to protect U.S. forces only when all other alternatives have failed. Defensive response may be made only after

actual hostile fire has been encountered and must be limited to an immediate response against only those forces actually firing at U.S. forces.

5. Air reconnaissance (manned and unmanned) and SIGINT operations are authorized throughout Laos, except as specified below:

    a. Manned tactical reconnaissance aircraft are not authorized to penetrate the NVN border, overfly Barrel Roll North or to fly within five kilometers of known or suspected Chinese positions in Barrel Roll West, unless approved by the JCS.

    b. High and low photo drones will not penetrate the NVN border, nor approach closer than 25 nautical miles to the PRC border.

    c. SR-71 and U-2 reconnaissance missions will not overfly the NVN border nor approach closer than ten nautical miles of the PRC border.

    d. Manned airborne SIGINT collection aircraft (other than SR-71 and U-2) operating over Laos will not penetrate the NVN border nor approach closer than 25 nautical miles to the PRC border.

6. Omitted.

7. SAR operations may be conducted for U.S. personnel throughout Laos. During the conduct of such operations, munitions expenditures, including RCA (CS), may be used under the terms of the defensive response provisions. SAR operations may be conducted in support of friendly aircrews in emergency situations when beyond RLAF capability.

8. Recovery of U.S. aircraft is authorized as required throughout Laos.

9. Omitted.

\*       \*       \*       \*       \*

(C) On 31 March, the positive control area (the area of Laos and Cambodia which bordered NVN and RVN) was reduced from ten nautical miles to five nautical miles in width.[74]

(TS) Even though a Laotian cease-fire had been declared and offensive operations had been terminated, the JCS, upon the request from the AmEmb Vientiane, approved a 72-hour offensive operations (nicknamed Prime Punch) which utilized B-52s and F-111s in the Vieng area, southeast of the Plaine des Jarres, on 15 April. The level of effort was to be from 21 to 30

B-52 and 30 F-111 sorties a day through the approved period or until lucrative targets no longer existed. TACAIR strikes were authorized if such use was necessary for successfully carrying out the overall mission.[75]

(C) In May and June, the only changes imposed upon 7AF OPORD 71-17 were those dealing with the inactivation of SOA-8, the clarification of target validation procedures in the approved operating areas, and the clarification of the positive control area.[76] There were no significant operational changes during this period.

(C) On 30 June 1973, the U.S. House of Representatives and the Senate agreed on the amendment to the joint resolution prohibiting funds to be obligated or expended for financing, directly or indirectly, combat activities by U.S. military forces in or over or from off the shores of NVN, RVN, Laos, or Cambodia. The funding prohibition was to be become effective on 15 August 1973 notwithstanding any other provisions of the law.[77]

(S) The only other change to the ROE prior to

the stop-the-bombing legislation was that in the positive control areas. All strikes, except B-52, F-111, and F-4 LORAN* pathfinding with approved all-weather bombing systems, were required to be conducted under the control of a FAC. All airstrikes in the PCA had to be planned and conducted in a manner that precluded the impact of ordnance in the RVN. The change again allowed airstrikes to within two nautical miles of the NVN border. Seventh Air Force was the approving authority for all strikes in the PCA.[78]

(TS) The passage of Public Law 93-50, with its stop-the-bombing amendment, on 1 July 1973 actually allowed operations to continue until 15 August 1973. With only a few exceptions, U.S. military operations of all types were prohibited in Laos after the latter date. (Refer to Appendix C for the complete operating authorities and Appendix D for the revised basic ROE which became effective on 150400Z August 1973.) On 14 September, CINCPAC prohibited all reconnaissance overflight of Laos[79] because a preliminary review of the Laotian peace protocols concluded that overflight by manned or unmanned reconnaissance vehicles was not

---

* (U) LORAN--Long range airborne navigation.

authorized, or, at best, left its legality unclear.[80] CINCPAC requested the JCS to confirm or correct this interpretation. The JCS replied that certain reconnaissance operations were required to be continued and did not violate the peace agreement. Accordingly, on 15 September 1973, Giant Scale and Buffalo Hunter operations over Laos were allowed to continue. All other reconnaissance platforms were prohibited from overflying Laotian territory.[81] On 21 September 1973, this restriction on reconnaissance operations was removed and the ROE concerning reconnaissance overflight reverted to the conditions imposed by the 15 August revised operating authorities (refer to Appendix C).[82]

CHAPTER V

<u>CAMBODIA</u>

(C)  U.S. Air Force involvement in the Khmer Republic during the period between October 1972 and January 1973 fluctuated in intensity, but remained relatively low overall.  The operating rules for aircraft, target validation procedures, and command and control relationships all remained essentially the same, with change occurring only in the level of effort.  This low level of activity was caused primarily by increased VC/NVA military efforts in South Vietnam which required the diversion of U.S. assets <u>from</u> the Khmer Republic.  The execution of Linebacker II operations in North Vietnam during December 1972 also required a high level of U.S. air participation and detracted from U.S. operations in the Khmer Republic.  It was not until January 1973 that changes began.  These were brought on by the Vietnam cease-fire, the unilateral cessation of offensive operations by Marshal Lon Nol, and the increased offensive actions by the Khmer insurgents (KI).[83]

The Southeast Asia operating authorities which became effective on 28 January, coincident with the cease-fire in Vietnam, had a section applicable to the Khmer Republic. Although many of the authorities on the validation and control of strikes in the Freedom Deal interdiction area remained unchanged, the complete operating authorities are listed:

TABLE 6

SEASIA OPERATING AUTHORITIES --
CEASE-FIRE RVN AND NVN (U)[84]

Note: In the event the Government of the Khmer Republic (GKR) suspends offensive military operations in Cambodia, separate guidance will be promulgated in the SPINs.

1. Search and Rescue (SAR).

(A) SAR operations for U.S. personnel may be conducted throughout Cambodia.

(B) In emergency situations beyond the capabilities of friendly air forces, SAR operations for friendly aircrews may be conducted throughout Cambodia.

(C) During the conduct of SAR operations, when necessary to protect the SAR forces and insure safe recovery of personnel:

(1) Ground fire may be returned.

(2) RCA (CS) may be employed throughout Cambodia.

(3) On a case-by-case basis, when determined by COMUSMACV/USSAG/7AF that such action is necessary, ground security forces may be employed in SAR efforts for U.S. personnel throughout Cambodia.

2. Recovery of U.S. aircraft is authorized in low risk areas throughout Cambodia.

3. Reconnaissance. Reconnaissance aircraft (manned and unmanned) are authorized to operate throughout Cambodia with armed escort as required.

4. Passive aerial operations. Inflight refueling, airborne early warning, command and control electronic warfare, radio relay, and the like are authorized in support of approved combat air operations.

5. Freedom Deal air interdiction area.

(A) Freedom Deal is as defined in 7AF OpOrd 71-17.

(B) TACAIR, Arc Light, and rotary and fixed wing gunships may conduct interdiction operations throughout Freedom Deal. Because of the denser population, strikes south of Route 13 are to be conducted only against confirmed highly lucrative targets that pose a substantial threat to Allied Forces.

6. Routes 3 and 4: TACAIR and Arc Light are authorized to support operations along and maintain the security of Cambodian Routes 3 and 4.

7. Mekong River: TACAIR, rotary and fixed wing gunships and rotary wing trooplift, MedEvac and logistic support are authorized for Mekong River security operations.

8. On a case-by-case basis, upon the recommendation of COMUSMACV/USSAG/7AF and when beyond the capability of Allied Forces, TACAIR may be employed throughout Cambodia in any situation which involves a serious threat to major Cambodian positions, the loss of which would constitute a military or psychological blow to the country.

9. Arc Light strikes may be conducted against targets in Cambodia south of the Freedom Deal area to the Gulf of Siam as approved by COMUSMACV/USSAG/7AF. Approval authority may be delegated to COMUSMACV/USSAG/7AF. CJCS will continue to be an information addressee on all strike requests and decisions to enable higher authority review prior to actual strike except in the case of last minute diverts necessary

to meet critical situations. Request all messages to Washington on this subject use Secret Limdis.

10. Flares: Flare operations are authorized as required within the Freedom Deal interdiction area; outside Freedom Deal flare operations may be conducted when no Vietnamese Air Force (VNAF), Khmer Air Force (KAF), or Royal Thai Air Force (RTAF) flare capability is available.

11. FAC: U.S. FACs may be employed to control RTAF, VNAF, and KAF airstrikes within areas where U.S. aircraft are authorized to conduct strikes. The specific target must have been validated by the ground commander. Immediate airstrikes must have been requested and positive communications must have been established between the ground command and FAC aircraft. Outside areas where U.S. aircraft are authorized to conduct strikes, they may provide passive support only as a communications link without active involvement.

12. U.S. forces are authorized to conduct PSYOPs against Viet Cong/North Vietnamese Army in an operational area including all of the Freedom Deal area,

a 50 kilometer strip from the southern edge of the Freedom Deal area to the Gulf of Thailand, paralleling the RVN border, and any areas where U.S. airstrikes have been authorized for a period of seven days following the airstrikes. In addition, public safety warnings may be disseminated to the Cambodian populace in all areas where airstrike operations are being conducted, and the assistance of the local populace may be solicited in areas suspected of harboring U.S. and Allied prisoners of war (POWs). For these purposes, printed media, loudspeakers, gift packages, and the use of U.S. aircraft and crews for the dissemination of materials are authorized. Phnom Penh, national monuments, shrines, and areas of cultural value to the Cambodian people are excluded from operational areas.

13. U.S. forces are authorized to provide support in the form of production and dissemination of printed material, to include delivery by U.S. aircraft and crews when requirements are beyond GKR capability.

14. Nothing in these authorities shall be construed as preventing any commander from taking such

action as may be necessary to defend his command.

*     *     *     *     *

(C) Two days later Secretary of State William P. Rogers directed the cessation of all U.S. TACAIR and B-52 strikes in order to give the unilateral cease-fire, directed by Marshal Lon Nol, every chance of success. While observing the spirit of the cease-fire, the JCS and the Secretary of State directed that the U. S. Ambassador to the Khmer Republic, Emory C. Swank, approve all airstrikes should such operations become necessary. Even if a proposed strike had complied with the standards imposed by the ROE and had been approved by Seventh Air Force, the Embassy still retained the authority for final approval, insuring the consideration of political factors. On 9 February 1973, the AmEmb Phnom Penh forwarded to Seventh Air Force the first request for limited U.S. air support. General John W. Vogt, Jr., Commander, Seventh Air Force, approved this request, but retained approval authority for each strike request.[85]

(TS) Because of the buildup of North Vietnamese supplies, equipment, and personnel in Freedom Deal and the need to counter specific hostile acts or threats against GKR forces, friendly populations, and facilities, the JCS suggested an expansion of the operating authorities in early March. On 9 March, the Ambassador and the Forces Armees Nationale Khmer (FANK) Chief of Staff approved the JCS authorities. These authorities permitted TACAIR and gunship strikes under FAC control throughout Freedom Deal without further clearance from the AmEmb Phnom Penh or the FANK. B-52 strikes were authorized throughout Freedom Deal, but required FANK approval through the AmEmb Phnom Penh. Because of the dense population, strikes south of Route 13 were to be conducted only against identified, highly lucrative targets that posed a threat to Allied forces. The prevalidated LOC structure (Category A and B LOCs) was reestablished in Freedom Deal, retaining the same limitations as before. Any strike outside Freedom Deal still required AmEmb validation.[86]

(C) On 31 March 1973, the AmEmb Phnom Penh removed two areas, one around Kampong Cham and the other around Kampong Thom, from the Freedom Deal area. The area around Kampong Cham extended from the western Freedom Deal border due east to Phum Chheuteal Khtuoy

(WU6060) and then due south to the Freedom Deal border. The exempted area around Kampong Thom was delineated by a line extending from the western Freedom Deal border east to WV2030, then south to WU2090, and then west to the Freedom Deal border. (Refer to Figure 7.) These areas were no longer considered to be in Freedom Deal. Any TACAIR strikes in these areas were required to be controlled by a FAC, using a ground commander and area control* for validation.[87]

(S) During March, the Khmer insurgents had gained control of sections of the bank of the Mekong River between Phnom Penh and the RVN border. The insecurity of the river forced the cancellation of some resupply convoys scheduled to travel up the river and resulted in a change in validation and control procedures for air operations in certain areas along the river. This area was designated as the Special Mekong Air Sector (SMAS) and was established, redefined, activated, and terminated as the situation dictated.[88]

---

*(C) Area control was a radio relay center in the AmEmb where USDAO personnel passed targeting information back and forth between Seventh Air Force command and control personnel and the FANK Combat Operations Center (COC) giving the Embassy's political approval for air strikes.

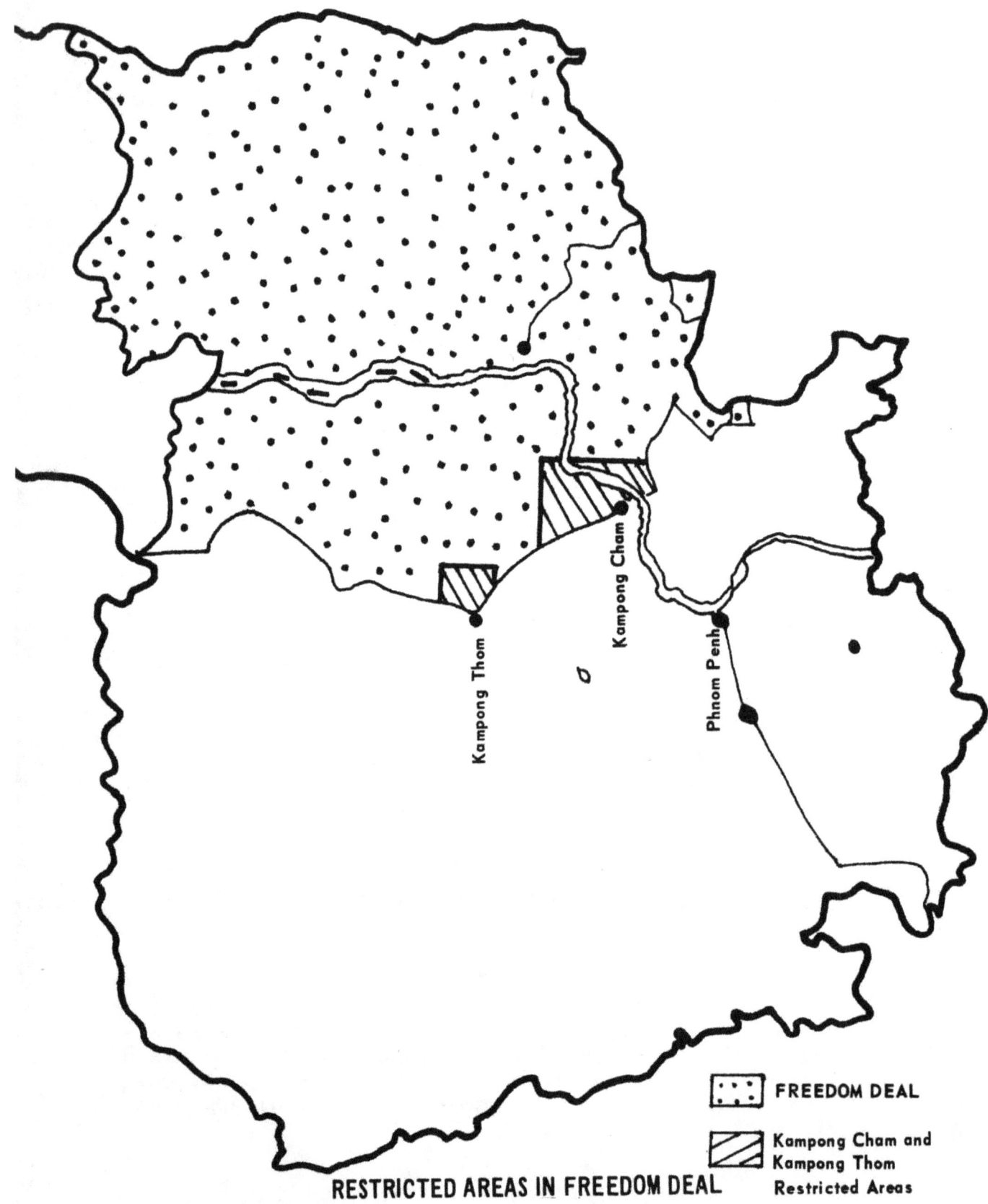

RESTRICTED AREAS IN FREEDOM DEAL

Brigadier General John R. D. Cleland, U.S. Army, Chief of the Military Equipment Delivery Team, Cambodia (CHMEDTC), proposed the concept on 1 April to General Vogt who concurred. General Vogt recommended, in addition, that the SMAS be declared a militarily critical area and that targets be validated accordingly.[89] The validation was to be accomplished by utilizing an airborne battlefield command and control center (ABCCC) aircraft. A FANK officer and an air attache representative would be aboard an ABCCC to prevalidate targets in order to comply with the JCS directives which required both AmEmb and GKR validation. The ABCCC aircraft commander was delegated Seventh Air Force authority to validate targets and approve the requested strikes in SMAS after FANK and AmEmb Phnom Penh validation was verified.[90] The First SMAS was established on 4 April, encompassing an area 15 kilometers on either side of the Mekong River, beginning just east of Phnom Penh and extending to the RVN border with an offset to the east to include the Prey Veng area.[91] The SMAS was to remain in effect until the critical military situation was terminated, at which time normal validation and approval procedures would again be in effect.[92]

(C) On 7 April 1975, USSAG/7AF rescinded a 9 March message which revalidated the Freedom Deal LOC structure and redefined Category A LOCs. The 1,000 meter limit on either side of the LOC remained in effect, but strikes were prohibited within 500 meters of an inhabited village without specific FANK validation. A FAC was required to control such strikes.[93] Seven days later OPS Supplement 149 was incorporated into the ROE which further defined the Category A LOC system. This supplement authorized strikes against targets or suspected targets as long as they were not otherwise prohibited by other current operating authorities. In addition, F-111s employing approved all-weather bombing systems were excluded from FAC control. All other TACAIR strikes remained under FAC control.[94]

(C) On 15 April, the special area around Kampong Cham, which had been established on 31 March, was reduced in size to about one-fourth of the original area. This policy decision largely reincorporated the exempted area into Freedom Deal. At the same time, the area around Kampong Thom was reduced by approximately one-half (refer to Figure 8). In these adjusted areas, Category A and B LOCs were no longer prevalidated for strikes. FACs were now required to obtain FANK, AmEmb Phnom Penh, and Seventh Air Force validation and approval prior to controlling TACAIR strikes; they were required to be in contact with the local ground commander and to have approval through area control. Those areas, which were again added to the Freedom Deal area, came under the administration of applicable Freedom Deal ROE.[95]

Because of the expanded air operations and the increase in the number of strikes, Ambassador Swank and General Vogt proposed to change the existing validation procedures.[96] Ambassador Swank, in a message to the SecState on 17 April, argued that the burden on the embassy staff (its members limited as they were by the Cooper-Church amendment) was too much to allow sufficient time for fully supporting target approval procedures. The Ambassador also stated that the Embassy would benefit from the ". . . political advantages of divorcing this mission (i.e., the U.S. Embassy) from

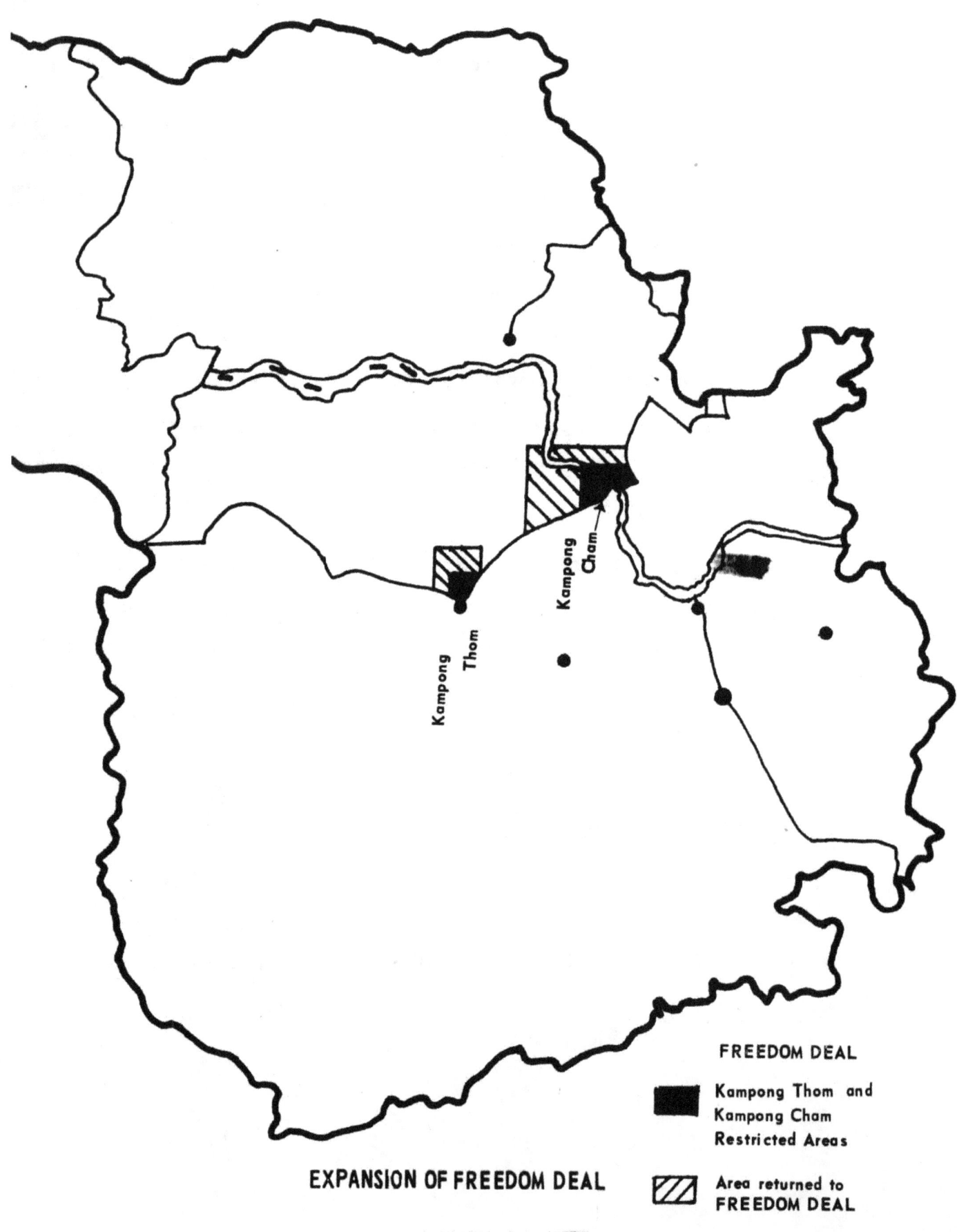

**EXPANSION OF FREEDOM DEAL**

FIGURE 8

an operational TACAIR role. . . ." This secondary reason might have been the real motivating factor for the AmEmbassy to seek a change in spite of ostensible appearances. Based upon a strong recommendation by the SecState to the JCS, the latter agreed to the elimination of the requirement for the AmEmb Phnom Penh's monthly approval of U.S. TACAIR support to FANK forces in areas outside Freedom Deal.[97]

(S) Operations under the new validation procedures became effective on 29 April. Target requests were routed from the ground commander to the FAC who passed the target information simultaneously to the Khmer Direct Air Support Center (KDASC)* and ABCCC. KDASC furnished the FANK validation while the ABCCC commander furnished Seventh Air Force validation. (All TACAIR target validation and approval authority, except F-111 beacon diverts, were given the ABCCC commander by the Commander, Seventh Air Force.)[98]

---

*(S) The KDASC was established in March 1973 to provide Khmer validation of targets outside Freedom Deal. It became fully operational in April and eventually replaced area control as the primary avenue by which Seventh Air Force received FANK target validation and air support requests.

(C) Later events showed how the new procedures were successful in streamlining the command and control for strikes. First reports indicated that the procedure had reduced target validation time by one-half. By the end of April, the new ABCCC target validation operations were so responsive to air support that the need for the SMAS ceased.[99]

In May, the designation of FANK ground commanders as forward air guides (FAGs) also helped to reduce the reaction time for air support. The FANK FAG could request air support either through the KDASC or a U.S. FAC and FANK validation of the target was inherent in the request. When a U.S. FAC received a request from a FAG, he forwarded the request to the ABCCC where the decision on the amount and type of support was made.[100] The extension of the AmEmb's blanket validation of TACAIR/gunship strikes through May and June was evidence of the success of the new procedures.[101]

(S) As the cease-fire planning progressed, the RVN PCA was activated. At the end of March, the PCA was reduced from ten nautical miles to five nautical miles in width.[102] In June, the PCA was further reduced to two nautical miles. The restriction was rescinded in August and maximum use of existing capabilities such as FAC and all-weather bombing systems was allowed when operating within five miles of the RVN border.[103]

(C) On 5 August, restricted area was established around Phnom Penh. All overflight of this restricted area was prohibited except B-52 flights at or above 30,000 feet. At the same time, the exception of FAC control in Freedom Deal for strikes on Category A and B LOCs and in special operating areas was rescinded. The only TACAIR expenditures which did not require FAC control were strikes by approved all-weather bombing systems and gunships which were authorized to "self-FAC."[104]

(S) On 11 August 1973, the JCS informed all military commands of the scheduled termination of "all acts of force initiated by U.S. forces in Cambodia" at 0400Z (1100 hours, Cambodia time) on 15 August 1973.[105] Operating authorities and rules of engagement which were to become effective with the 15 August cease-fire

were promulgated on 14 August and distributed to all
SEA units. The authorities and ROE were basically the
same as those established for the RVN and Laos when
the cease-fires became effective in those areas.
Defensive response was established to protect U.S.
forces only when other alternatives failed. Immediate
pursuit was authorized when U.S. forces came under
attack and was essential for self-defense. Overflight of the Khmer Republic was authorized in certain
cases for supporting noncombat operations. Manned
and unmanned, unarmed, tactical reconnaissance was
authorized throughout the Khmer Republic pending the
resolution of diplomatic issues. Certain operations
connected with SAR, PSYOP, logistics, use of airbases,
crash/grave site inspections, evacuation, escort, and
training were authorized.[106] The extent to which these
operations were allowed is described in Appendixes
C and D (the operating authorities and ROE were effective on 150400Z August 1973).

## CHAPTER VI

### SUMMARY

(U) From October 1972 through August 1973, the changes in the ROE may be seen as reflecting the changing tenor of the negotiations for peace in SEA. This connection is most clearly seen in the modifications of the ROE affecting the Republic of Vietnam and North Vietnam during the period preceding the signing of the cease-fire in Vietnam. As the North Vietnamese seriously undertook negotiations, the ROE were made restrictive thereby reducing the level of air operations. When they lacked sincerity in their discussions in Paris, the ROE were loosened to allow great pressure to be applied by increased air operations. The Linebacker II campaign in December 1972 was a classic example of the relationship between U.S. national policy -- the constraints of which were reflected in the rules of engagement -- and military operations supporting that policy. When the enemy refused to negotiate and reneged on many of the protocols which had been accepted, the United States unleased its powerful forces. The removal of many of the bombing restrictions during Linebacker II paved the way for the nearly unrestricted use of air power. The Linebacker II campaign lasted only twelve days, but the awesome destruction wreaked by U.S. power persuaded a chastened Hanoi to return to the negotiating table. As the peace negotiations drew to a successful close, the most restrictive ROE were circumscribed about air operations, culminating in the termination of all U.S. offensive operations in both Vietnams with the signing of the peace agreement on 27 January 1973.

The application of the ROE in Laos followed the pattern of their use in the Republic of Vietnam and North Vietnam. With the signing of the Paris agreement for ending the war in North and South Vietnam, the ROE were altered to constrain air operations in Laos. Most of the restrictions were intended to strengthen the buffer zone between Laos and North Vietnam. After 27 January 1973, the buffer zone became increasingly important. The main reason for prohibiting strikes in the buffer zone was to prevent the inadvertent penetration of NVN airspace. Such a penetration would have been a violation of the peace agreement and, needless to say, would have caused problems in maintaining an already shaky cease-fire. On 22 February 1973, the Laotian cease-fire became effective and U.S. operations were restricted in that country. Laos became a restricted area; U.S. aircraft could approach no closer than five nautical miles of the Laotian border from any bordering country. As with the buffer zone for North Vietnam, this restricted area was to prevent aircraft operating in Cambodia and Thailand from the unauthorized overflight of Laos. Except for Operation Prime Punch, U.S. operations in Laos between the beginning of the Laotian cease-fire and the total bombing halt in August 1973 were limited to reconnaissance and ELINT responses to aggressive actions by the Communists.

Operations in the Khmer Republic remained at a relatively low level throughout the latter part of 1972 and into January 1973. Two days after the NVN/RVN cease-fire became effective, U.S. airstrikes in the Khmer Republic were stopped. This was to support the unilateral cease-fire undertaken by the Khmer Government. However, less than two weeks after the unilateral cease-fire, U.S. operations were again approved for the Khmer Republic. The level of U.S. operations continued to increase throughout the Khmer Republic until 15 August 1973 when all acts of force by the United States in the GKR and other parts of SEA were terminated.

(S) The ROE for the RVN, Laos, and the Khmer Republic became basically the same on 15 August. All offensive operations were prohibited. The procedures for defensive response were established and overflight during certain operations was approved. After August 1973, operations in SEA could only be defensive in nature and only in response to hostile acts by the enemy. The operating authorities and ROE effective after 15 August are listed in Appendixes C and D.

(S) In February 1974, USSAG/7AF promulgated USSAG/7AF OPORD 74-01. This operational order superseded 7AF OPORD 71-17 and defined the ROE to apply in the event of renewed hostilities in SEA. The new ROE were for contingency planning and training purposes only; they would become effective as combat ROE only when specifically directed by the COMUSSAG/7AF.[107]

APPENDIX A

SOUTHEAST ASIA BASIC RULES OF ENGAGEMENT (ROE)
CEASE-FIRE IN RVN AND NVN EFFECTIVE 272359Z JANUARY 1973*

1. (C) Definitions:

   a. (C) Southeast Asia (SEA): For purposes of these rules, SEA includes the airspaces, land mass, and territorial/internal waters of:

   (1) Thailand, Laos, Khmer Republic (GKR), North Vietnam (NVN), and the Republic of Vietnam (RVN).

   (2) The international waters and airspace of:

   (a) The Gulfs of Siam and Tonkin,

   (b) The South China Sea,

in or over which U.S. forces operate in relation to U.S. objectives in SEA.

   b. (C) Territorial seas: A belt of sea adjacent to a coastal state three nautical miles in breadth, measured from the low watermark along the coast. However, in the states claiming over three miles of territorial seas, that claimed distance shall be observed for these rules as if it were the width of their territorial seas, but not to exceed 12 nautical miles in any case. The following are the states' claims with regard to territorial sea:

---

*From a message (S-GDS-83), JCS to CINCPAC, CINCSAC, subj: SEAsia Basic Rules of Engagement (ROE)--Cease-fire in RVN and NVN (U), 270703Z Jan 1973. (CMR TS-222, 027)

(1) Thailand--12 miles.

(2) Khmer Republic--12 miles.

(3) RVN--Three miles.

(4) NVN--12 miles.

(5) People's Republic of China (PRC)--12 miles.

c. (U) Internal waters: Waters to landward of the territorial sea.

d. (U) Territorial airspace: Airspace above the land territory, internal waters, and territorial seas of a sovereign country.

e. (C) Friendly forces: Includes all free world military assistance (FWMA), South Vietnamese, Royal Thai (RTG), Royal Laotian (RLG), and Khmer air, ground, and naval units operating with these forces to include such quasi-official organizations as Air America.

f. (C) Hostile aircraft (RVN and Thailand):

(1) An aircraft which is visually identified or is designated by the Director of a U.S. Air Operations Center, or his authorized U.S. representative, as an NVN aircraft operating in RVN or Thai territorial airspace without proper clearance from the government concerned, or

(2) An aircraft observed in one of the following acts:

(a) Attacking, or acting in a manner which indicates with reasonable certainty an intent to attack U.S./friendly forces or installations.

(b) Laying mines, without permission of the government concerned within or immediately adjacent to territorial seas or internal waters.

(c) Releasing free drops, parachutes, or gliders over or immediately adjacent to friendly territory/territorial airspace/seas when obviously not in distress and without permission of government concerned. This includes the unauthorized landing of troops or materiel.

g. (C) Hostile aircraft (Laos as agreed to by RLG and Khmer Republic).

(1) Any positively identified NVN combat aircraft (fighter/bombers, bomber, or interceptor) or

(2) Any aircraft designated hostile by the U.S. Director of a TACC (Tactical Air Control Center)/ADCC (Air Defense Control Center/ACC (Air Control Center) or his authorized representative, or

(3) Any aircraft attacking or acting in a manner which indicates with reasonable certainty, intent to attack U.S./friendly forces or installations, or

(4) Any aircraft laying mines, releasing free drops, parachutes or gliders in support of unfriendly forces, including unauthorized landing of troops or materiel.

h. (C) Hostile vessel (surface or submarine);

(1) A vessel in RVN - Khmer - Thai internal waters and/or

territorial seas or Southeast Asian international waters which is engaged in one of the following acts:

(a) Attacking or acting in a manner which indicates with reasonable certainty an intent to attack U.S./friendly forces or installations; including the unauthorized landing of troops or materiel on friendly territory.

(b) Laying mines within friendly territorial seas or internal waters without permission of the government concerned.

(c) Engaged in direct support of attacks against RVN, Khmer Republic, or Thailand;

(2) A vessel in Laos' internal waters which attacks U.S./friendly forces (when agreed to by RLG).

i. (C) Proper clearances: An aircraft, vessel, vehicle, or force clearance, granted by authorized agencies of the government concerned, for entry into specific areas of its territory, internal waters, territorial seas, or territorial airspace.

j. (C) Hostile ground forces (RVN-Thailand-Laos-Khmer Republic): Ground forces which attack U.S./friendly forces, facilities, or population centers.

k. (C) Immediate pursuit: Pursuit initiated in response to actions or attacks by hostile aircraft or vessels as defined in these ROE. The pursuit must be continuous and uninterrupted and may be continued as necessary and feasible in international and territorial airspace/seas or in internal waters as prescribed herein.

1. (C) Attacks:

(1) Major attack: One in which U.S./friendly forces, facilities, or population centers:

(a) Receive numerous rounds of enemy mortar, artillery or rocket fire within a short period of time or sporadically over a period of hours.

(b) Receive a multi-company ground attack with or without supporting fire.

(c) Are subjected to one or more acts of terrorism involving extensive use of mines and demolitions.

(2) Minor attack: One in which U.S./friendly forces, facilities, or population centers:

(a) Receive one or a very few rounds of enemy mortar, artillery, rocket, or small arms fire following an extended period during which no stand-off attacks by fire are received.

(b) Receive a small ground probe, unsupported by significant mortar, artillery, or rocket fire, following an extended period during which no attacks of this type are received.

(c) Are subjected to one or a very few small terrorist attacks involving use of mines and demolitions following an extended period during which no attacks of this type are received.

 (3) Attack against aircraft and vessels: One in which U.S./friendly aircraft or vessels:

  (a) Receive enemy antiaircraft or coastal defense artillery, rocket, or missile fire, or

  (b) Receive fire of any sort from hostile aircraft or vessels as defined in these Rules of Engagement.

2. (C) <u>General Rules</u>:

 a. (C) U.S. forces operating in SEA are authorized to attack and destroy any hostile aircraft or vessels as herein defined; except where operating authorities, promulgated separately, limit this authority or preclude introduction of U.S. forces into the area.

 b. (C) U.S. forces in SEA are authorized to attack and destroy hostile ground forces, as herein defined, which attack U.S. personnel in RVN or U.S. friendly forces, facilities, materiel, or population centers in Laos, or the Khmer Republic.

 c. (C) Immediate pursuit may be conducted as necessary and feasible pursuant to the above, subject to the following conditions and limitations:

  (1) In the event U.S. forces are attacked by hostile forces in the RVN, Laos, Thailand, NVN, Khmer Republic, or Southeast Asian international waters/airspace, U.S. forces may conduct immediate pursuit

into international waters/airspace or territorial seas/airspace of the RVN, Thailand, NVN, Laos, and Khmer Republic;

(2) No pursuit is authorized into the territorial seas and airspace of the People's Republic of China.

(3) U.S. forces which, under the limitations of these rules, enter unfriendly territorial seas or airspace in immediate pursuit, are not authorized to attack other unfriendly forces or installations encountered, unless attacked first by them, and then only to the extent necessary for self-defense.

(4) Declaration of aircraft or vessels as hostile will be tempered with judgment and discretion. Cases can occur wherein the destruction of aircraft and vessels would be contrary to U.S. and Allied interests. All available information and intelligence shall be considered in determining action to be taken in such cases. Examples include:

(a) Properly cleared aircraft and vessels engaged in cease-fire monitoring or resupply operating in RVN, Khmer, Thai, or Lao territory, internal waters, territorial airspace/seas, but wherein the official authorized to declare aircraft or vessels as hostile is not in receipt of the proper clearance.

(b) Civilian aircraft or vessels operating without proper clearance in RVN, Khmer, Thai, or Lao territory, internal waters, territorial airspace/seas due to navigational error.

(c) Aircraft or vessels manned by defectors attempting to land in order to seek asylum.

3. (U) Nothing in these rules modifies in any manner the requirement of a military commander to defend his unit against armed attack with all means at his disposal. In the event of such attack, the commander concerned will take immediate, aggressive action against the attacking force.

APPENDIX B

## SOUTHEAST ASIA BASIC RULES OF ENGAGEMENT (ROE) CEASE-FIRE IN NVN, RVN, THE DMZ AND LAOS (U)*

(U) The following basic ROE will govern operations of U.S. forces in Southeast Asia (SEA) following the cease-fire in Laos which is effective 220500Z February 1973.

1. (C) <u>Definitions</u>:

    a. (C) SEA: For purposes of these rules, SEA includes the airspace, land mass, and territorial/internal waters of:

        (1) Thailand, Laos, Khmer Republic, North Vietnam, and the Republic of Vietnam.

        (2) The international waters and airspace of:

            (a) The Gulfs of Siam and Tonkin.

            (b) The South China Sea, in or over which U.S. forces operate in relation to U.S. objectives in SEA.

    b. (C) Territorial seas: A belt of sea adjacent to a coastal state three nautical miles in breadth, measured from the low watermark along the coast. However, in the states claiming over three miles of territorial seas, that claimed distance shall be observed for these

---

*From a message (S-GDS-83), JCS to CINCPAC, CINCSAC, subj: SEAsia Basic Rules of Engagement (ROE)--Cease-fire in NVN, RVN, the DMZ and Laos (U), 212332Z Feb 1973. (CMR TS-222, 024)

rules as if it were the width of their territorial seas, but not to exceed 12 nautical miles in any case. The following are the states' claims with regard to territorial sea:

    (1) Thailand--12 miles.

    (2) Khmer Republic--12 miles.

    (3) RVN--Three miles.

    (4) NVN--12 miles.

    (5) PRC--12 miles.

  c. (U) Internal waters: Waters to landward of the territorial sea.

  d. (U) Territorial airspace: Airspace above the land territory, internal waters, and territorial seas of a sovereign country.

  e. (C) Friendly forces: Includes all free world military assistance, RVN, Royal Thai, Royal Laotian, and Khmer air, ground, and naval units operating with these forces to include such quasi-official organizations as Air America.

  f. (C) Hostile aircraft (in Thailand and Laos as agreed to by RLG and Thailand).

    (1) An aircraft which is visually identified or is designated by the Director of a U.S. Air Operations Center, or his authorized U.S. representative as an NVN aircraft operating in RVN, Lao, or Thai territorial airspace without proper clearance from the government concerned, or

(2) An aircraft observed in one of the following acts:

(a) Attacking, or acting in a manner which indicates with reasonable certainty an intent to attack U.S./friendly forces or installations.

(b) Laying mines, without permission of the government concerned, within or immediately adjacent to territorial seas or internal waters.

(c) Releasing free drops, parachutes, or gliders over or immediately adjacent to friendly territory/territorial airspace/seas when obviously not in distress and without permission of the government concerned. This includes the unauthorized landing of troops or materiel.

g. (C) Hostile aircraft (Khmer Republic):

(1) Any positively identified NVN combat aircraft fighter/bomber, bomber, or interceptor, or

(2) Any aircraft designated hostile by the U.S. Director of a TACC/ADCC/ADC or his authorized representative or,

(3) Any aircraft attacking or acting in a manner which indicates with reasonable certainty, intent to attack U.S./friendly forces or installations or

(4) Any aircraft laying mines, releasing free drops, parachutes or gliders in support of unfriendly forces, including unauthorized landing of troops or materiel.

h.  (C)  Hostile vessel (surface or subsurface):

(1)  A vessel in RVN - Khmer - Thai internal waters and/or territorial seas or Southeast Asian international waters which is engaged in one of the following acts:

(a)  Attacking or acting in a manner which indicates with reasonable certainty, intent to attack U.S./friendly forces or installations including the unauthorized landing of troops or materiel on friendly territory.

(b)  Laying mines within friendly territorial seas or internal waters without permission of the government concerned.

(c)  Engaged in direct support of attacks against RVN, Khmer Republic, or Thailand.

(2)  A vessel in Laos internal waters which attacks U.S./friendly forces (when agreed to by RLG).

i.  (C)  Proper clearances:  An aircraft, vessel, vehicle, or force clearance, granted by authorized agencies of the government concerned, for entry into specific areas of its territory, internal waters, territorial seas, or territorial airspace.

j.  (C)  Hostile ground forces (RVN, Thailand, Laos, Khmer Republic):  Ground forces which attack U.S./friendly forces facilities, or population centers.

k.  (C)  Immediate pursuit:  Pursuit initiated in response to actions or attacks by hostile aircraft or vessels as defined in these

ROE. The pursuit must be continuous and uninterrupted and may be continued as necessary and feasible in international and territorial airspace/seas or in internal waters.

1. (C) Attacks:

(1) Major attack: One in which U.S./friendly forces, facilities or population centers:

(a) Receive numerous rounds of enemy mortar, artillery or rocket fire within a short period of time or sporadically over a period of hours.

(b) Receive a multi-company ground attack with or without supporting fire.

(c) Are subjected to one or more acts of terrorism involving extensive use of mines and demolitions.

(2) Minor attack: One in which U.S./friendly forces, facilities or population centers:

(a) Receive one or a very few rounds of enemy mortar, artillery rocket, or small arms fire following an extended period during which no stand-off attacks by fire are received.

(b) Receive a small ground probe, unsupported by significant mortar, artillery, or rocket fire, following an extended period during which no attacks of this type are received.

(c) Are subjected to one or a very few small terrorist attacks involving use of mines and demolitions following an extended period during which no attacks of this type are received.

  (3) Attack against aircraft and vessels: One in which U.S./friendly aircraft or vessels:

   (a) Receive enemy antiaircraft or coastal defense artillery rocket, or missile fire, or

   (b) Receive fire of any sort from hostile aircraft or vessels, as defined in these Rules of Engagement.

2. (C) <u>General Rules</u>:

 a. (C) U.S. forces operating in SEA are authorized to attack and destroy any hostile aircraft or vessel as herein defined, except where operating authorities, promulgated separately, limit this authority or preclude introduction of U.S. forces into the area.

 b. (C) U.S. forces in SEA are authorized to attack and destroy hostile ground forces, as herein defined, which attack U.S. personnel in RVN or Laos or U.S. friendly forces, facilities, materiel, or population centers in the Khmer Republic.

 c. (C) Immediate pursuit may be conducted as necessary and feasible pursuant to the above, subject to the following conditions and limitations:

  (1) In the event U.S. forces are attacked by hostile forces in the RVN, Laos, Thailand, NVN, Khmer Republic, or Southeast Asian international waters/airspace or territorial seas/airspace,

U.S. forces may conduct immediate pursuit into international waters/ airspace or territorial seas/airspace of the RVN, Thailand, NVN, Laos, and Khmer Republic.

(2) No pursuit is authorized into the territorial seas or airspace of the PRC.

(3) U.S. forces which, under the limitations of these rules enter unfriendly territorial sea or airspace in immediate pursuit, are not authorized to attack other unfriendly forces or installations encountered unless attacked first by them, and then only to the extent necessary for self-defense.

(4) Declaration of aircraft or vessels as hostile will be tempered with judgment and discretion. Cases can occur wherein the destruction of aircraft and vessels would be contrary to U.S. and Allied interests. All available information and intelligence shall be considered in determining action to be taken in such cases. Examples include:

(a) Properly cleared aircraft and vessels engaged in cease-fire monitoring or resupply operating in RVN, Khmer Republic, Thailand, or Laos territory, internal waters, territorial airspace seas, but wherein the official authorized to declare aircraft or vessels as hostile is not in receipt of the proper clearance.

(b) Civilian aircraft or vessels operating without proper clearance in RVN, Khmer, Thai, or Lao territory, internal waters, territorial airspace/seas due to navigational error.

    (c) Aircraft or vessels manned by defectors attempting to land in order to seek asylum.

  3. (U) Nothing in these rules modifies in any manner the requirement of a military commander to defend his unit against armed attack with all means at his disposal. In the event of such attack, the commander concerned will take immediate, aggressive action against the attacking forces.

## APPENDIX C

## SOUTHEAST ASIA OPERATING AUTHORITIES - CEASE-FIRE IN NVN, RVN, THE DMZ, LAOS AND CESSATION OF COMBAT ACTIVITIES BY US FORCES IN GKR*

1. (S) U.S. military operations of all types are prohibited throughout the territory, territorial airspace/seas of North and South Vietnam, Laos, and Cambodia, except as specifically authorized below:

    a. (S) Defensive responses: In the event U.S. forces are fired upon while conducting approved operations in or over North or South Vietnam, Laos, or Cambodia, every effort will be made to disengage. Defensive responses are authorized to protect U.S. forces only when other alternatives have failed. Defensive response may be made only after actual hostile fire has been encountered and must be limited to an immediate response against only those forces actually firing at U.S. forces. Defensive responses will not be initiated solely in response to activation of hostile radars.

    b. Immediate pursuit: When U.S. forces are under attack, they may, if essential for self-defense, conduct immediate pursuit of attacking forces into the territorial waters or airspace of North or South Vietnam, Laos, or Cambodia. Immediate pursuit must be continuous and uninterrupted and is authorized only to protect U.S. forces, and only

---

*From a message (S-GDS-83), USSAG/7AF to AIG 789, subj: SEAsia Operating Authorities (U), 151030Z Aug 1973. (CMR TS-222, 039)

until the hostile aircraft or vessels no longer pose an immediate threat. Immediate pursuit shall not include prolonged pursuit deep into hostile airspace. U.S. forces in immediate pursuit are authorized to attack other forces or installations encountered, only when attacked first by them, and then only to the extent necessary for self-defense.

  c. (C) Overflight: Overflight of South Vietnam, Laos, and Cambodia is authorized as necessary for the conduct of approved administrative logistics and noncombat support operations in Southeast Asia (SEA). Overflight of North Vietnam for any purpose is prohibited, except courier and ICCS support flights approved by AmEmb Saigon and cleared by the DRV [Democratic Republic of Vietnam].

  d. (S) Reconnaissance: Unarmed aerial reconnaissance and the support thereof are authorized as required throughout Laos, South Vietnam, and Cambodia, except as specified below:

  (1) Manned tactical reconnaissance aircraft are not authorized to penetrate the NVN border, overfly Barrel Roll North, or to fly within five kilometers of known or suspected Chinese positions in Barrel Roll East or Barrel Roll West, unless approved by JCS.

  (2) High and low photo drones will not penetrate the NVN border nor approach closer than 25 nautical miles of the PRC border.

  (3) SR-71 and U-2 reconnaissance missions will not overfly the NVN border nor approach closer than ten nautical miles to the PRC border.

(4) Manned airborne SIGINT collection aircraft (other than SR-71 and U-2) operating over Laos will not penetrate the NVN border nor approach closer than 25 nautical miles to the PRC border.

e. (S) Search and rescue: Search and rescue operations may be conducted for U.S. personnel throughout SEA. During conduct of such operations, munitions expenditures, including riot control agent (RCA) [tear gas], must be conducted only under the terms of defensive response as outlined in paragraph 1a, above.

f. (C) Recovery of aircraft: Recovery of downed U.S. aircraft is authorized throughout South Vietnam, Laos, and Cambodia. In areas controlled by North Vietnamese Army/Viet Cong/Pathet Lao/Khmer insurgent (NVA/VC/PL/KI) forces, or in the contested areas of Southeast Asia, recovery of aircraft will be arranged in accordance with procedures provided separately. No recovery of U.S. aircraft from North Vietnam is authorized without approval from higher authority.

g. (S) Psychological operations (psyop):

(1) U.S. forces are authorized to conduct psyop against VC, NVA, and KI target audiences throughout Cambodia. For these purposes, printed media, gift packages and use of U.S. aircraft and crews for dissemination of materials are approved, except where serious risk to aircraft and crew is involved. Moreover, while Phnom Penh, national monuments, shrines, and areas of cultural value to the Cambodian people are excluded from operational areas, the authorization does

(c) Are subjected to one or more acts of terrorism involving extensive use of mines and demolitions.

(2) Minor attack: One in which U.S. forces or facilities:

(a) Receive one or a very few rounds of enemy mortar, artillery rocket, or small arms fire following an extended period during which no standoff attacks by fire were received.

(b) Receive a small ground probe, unsupported by significant mortar, artillery, or rocket fire, following an extended period during which no attacks of this type were received.

(c) Are subjected to one or a very few, small terrorist attacks involving use of mines and demolitions following an extended period during which no attacks of this type were received.

(3) Attack against aircraft and vessels: One in which U.S. aircraft or vessels:

(a) Receive enemy antiaircraft or coastal defense artillery, rocket, or mission fire, or:

(b) Receive fire of any sort from hostile aircraft or vessels as defined in these ROE.

2. (C) <u>General Rules</u>:

a. (C) U.S. forces operating in SEA are authorized to attack and destroy any hostile aircraft or vessel as herein defined, except where operating authorities promulgated separately limit this authority or preclude introduction of U.S. forces into the area.

b. (C) U.S. forces in SEA are authorized to attack and destroy hostile ground forces, as herein defined, which attack U.S. personnel in RVN, Laos, or Khmer Republic.

c. (C) Immediate pursuit may be conducted as necessary and feasible pursuant to the above, subject to the following conditions and limitations.

(1) In the event U.S. forces are attacked by hostile forces in the RVN, Laos, Thailand, NVN, the Khmer Republic, or SEA international waters/airspace or territorial seas/airspace of the RVN, Laos, Thailand, and the Khmer Republic.

(2) No pursuit is authorized into territorial seas or airspace of the People's Republic of China (PRC).

(3) U.S. forces which under the limitations of these rules, enter unfriendly territorial seas or airspace in immediate pursuit, are not authorized to attack other unfriendly forces or installations encountered, unless attacked first by them and then only to the extent necessary for self-defense.

(4) Declaration of aircraft or vessels as hostile will be tempered with judgment and discretion, cases can occur wherein the destruction of aircraft and vessels would be contrary to U.S. and Allied interests. All available information and intelligence shall be considered in determining action to be taken in such cases. Examples include:

(a) Properly cleared aircraft and vessels engaged in cease-fire monitoring or resupply operating in RVN, GKR, Thai, or Lao territory, internal waters, territorial airspace/seas, but wherein the official authorized to declare aircraft or vessels hostile is not in receipt of proper clearance.

(b) Civilian aircraft or vessels operating without proper clearance in RVN, GKR, Thai, or Lao territory, internal waters, territorial airspace/seas due to navigational error.

(c) Aircraft or vessels manned by defectors attempting to land in order to seek asylum.

3. (U) Nothing in these authorities shall be construed as precluding a commander from using all means at his disposal to exercise the inherent right and responsibility to conduct operations for self-defense of his forces.

NOTES

1. The Department of State Bulletin (U), "U.S. Foreign Policy for the 1970s, Shaping a Durable Peace," by Richard M. Nixon to the Congress on 3 May 1973, dated 4 Jun 73, p. 737. (Hereafter cited as Dept of State Bulletin, 4 Jun 73.)

2. Project CHECO Report (S-GDS-83), Rules of Engagement, November 1969-September 1972 (U), 1 Mar 73, p. 1. (Hereafter cited as ROE, Nov 69-Sep 72.) (CHECO Microfilm Roll CMR TS-183, 088) Material used is unclassified.

3. 7AF OPORD 71-17 (S-XCL-3), Rules of Engagement (U), DOCC, 6 Dec 71, Sec. 1. (Hereafter cited as 7AF OPORD 71-17.) (CMR S-729, 096)

4. Ibid.

5. Ibid., Sec. II, RVN. (CMR S-729, 098)

6. ROE, Nov 69-Sep 72 (S-GDS-83), p. 6.

7. Ibid., p. 32.

8. Ibid., p. 47.

9. Project CHECO Report (S-GDS-83), Linebacker: Overview of the First 120 Days (U), 27 Sep 73, pp. 15-18. (CMR TS-195, 119)

10. ROE, Nov 69-Sep 72 (S-GDS-83), pp. 48-49.

11. Ibid., pp. 8-9.

12. U.S. MACV Command History, January 1972-March 1973 (TS-XGDS- 2&3), Vol 1, pp. B-22, B-23. (CMR TS-232, 024)

13. ROE, Nov 69-Sep 72 (S-GDS-83), pp. 14-16.

14. Ibid., pp. 15-17.

15. Ibid., pp. 20-22.

16. Ibid., pp. 27-29.

17. Msg (TS-XGDS-3), JCS to CINCPAC, Subj: SEAsia Operating Authorities (U), 301619Z Oct 72. (CMR TS-222, 020)

18. Ibid.

19. Msg (TS-XGDS-3), JCS to CINCPAC, Subj: Temporary SEAsia Operating Authorities (U), 292353Z Nov 72, retransmitted by CINCPAC to CINCUSARPAC, CINCPACAF et al., 302223Z Nov 72.

20. Msg (TS-XGDS-3), JCS to CINCPAC, Subj: Air Activity Authorities (U), 060045Z Nov 72. (CMR TS-172, 078)

21. Dept of State Bulletin, 4 Jun 73, p. 744.

22. Msg (S-GDS-83), JCS to CINCPAC, Subj: SE Asia Operating Authorities--Cease-Fire in RVN and NVN (U), 240456Z Jan 73, referenced in msg (S-GDS-83), JCS to CINCPAC and CINCSAC, Subj: Revised SE Asia Operating Authorities (AOA) (U), 142336Z Aug 73. (CMR TS-222, 09)

23. Msg (TS-XGDS-3), JCS to CINCPAC, Subj: SE Asia Operating Authorities-- Cease-Fire in RVN and NVN (U), 270657Z Jan 73. (CMR TS-222, 024)

24. Msg (S-GDS-82), CINCPAC to COMUSMACV, CINCPACFLT, et al., Subj: Change 2 to Linebacker/Blue Tree Basic Operations Order (U), 112231Z Oct 72. (CMR TS-222, 018)

25. Ibid.

26. Dept of State Bulletin (U), 4 June 73, p. 743.

27. Msg (S-GDS-82), JCS to CINCPAC, Subj: Operations in NVN (U), 221956Z Oct 72. (CMR TS-157, 195)

28. Dept of State Bulletin (U), 4 June 73, p. 743.

29. Ibid.

30. Msg (TS-XGDS-3), JCS to CINCPAC and CINCSAC, Subj: Operating Authorities--SE Asia (U), 022247Z Nov 72, retransmitted by CINCPAC to COM 7AF, COMSEVENTHFLT, et al., 040304Z Nov 72. (CMR TS-168,037)

31. Msg (TS-XGDS-3), JCS to CINCPAC and CINCSAC, Subj: Operating Authorities--SE Asia (U), 042127Z Nov 72. (CMR TS-172, 120)

32. Msg (TS-XGDS-3), JCS to CINCPAC, Subj: B-52 Operating Authorities (U), 020231Z Nov 72. (CMR TS-168, 028)

33. Msg (TS-XGDS-3), JCS to CINCPAC, Subj: B-52 Operating Authorities (U), 050045Z Nov 72. (CMR TS-173, 051)

34. Dept of State Bulletin (U), 4 June 73, p. 744.

35. Msg (TS-XGDS-3), JCS to CINCPAC and CINCSAC, Subj: Linebacker II Operations (U), 170010Z Dec 72. (CMR TS-184, 065)

36. Msg (TS-XGDS-3), JCS to CINCPAC and CINCSAC, Subj: SEA Combat Operations (U), 192322Z Dec 72. (CMR TS-184, 070)

37. Msg (TS-XGDS-3), JCS to CINCPAC and CINCSAC, Subj: Linebacker II Operations (U), 170010Z Dec 72. (CMR TS-184, 065)

38. Msg (TS-XGDS-3), JCS to CINCPAC and CINCSAC, Subj: Linebacker II--Post Christmas Operations (S), 232247Z Dec 72. (CMR TS-184, 082)

39. Msg (S-GDS-82), JCS to CINCPAC and CINCSAC, no subj (Linebacker II), 291407Z Dec 72. (CMR TS-184, 089)

40. Msg (S-GDS-82), JCS to CINCPAC and CINCSAC, no subj (Linebacker II), 291407Z Dec 72. (CMR TS-184, 089)

41. Dept of State Bulletin (U), 4 June 73, p. 745.

42. Msg (TS-XGDS-2), JCS to CINCPAC and CINCSAC, Subj: Operations Against North Vietnam (U), 150356Z Jan 73. (CMR TS-214, 083)

43. Ibid.

44. Msg (C-GDS-81), 7AF to AIG 7939, Subj: Positive Control Area/Positive Control Zone (U), 161005Z Jan 73. (CMR S-951, 004)

45. Dept of State Bulletin (U), 4 June 73, p. 745.

45a. Msg (TS-XGDS-3), JCS to CINCPAC, Subj: SE Asia Operating Authorities--Cease-Fire in RVN and NVN (U), 270657Z Jan 73. (CMR TS-222, 024)

46. ROE, Nov 69-Sep 72 (S), p. 8.

47. Dept of State Bulletin (U), 4 June 73, p. 751.

48. Msg (TS-XGDS-3), JCS to CINCPAC and CINCSAC, Subj: SE Asia Operating Authorities (U), 301619Z Oct 72. (CMR TS-222, 020)

48a. Ibid.

49. Msg (TS-XGDS-3), JCS to CINCPAC and CINCSAC, Subj: Temporary SE Asia Operating Authorities (U), 292353Z Nov 72, retransmitted by CINCPAC to COM 7AF, 302223Z Nov 72. (CMR TS-203, 081)

50. Msg (C-GDS-80), 7AF to AIG 789, Subj: Ops Supplement 97 to 7AF OPORD 71-17 (U), 010220Z Nov 72. (CMR S-807, 109)

51. Msg (C/NOFORN-GDS-80), OUSAIRA Vientiane to 7AF, 7/13AF, et al., Subj: Armed Recce (U), 020945Z Nov 72. (CMR S-807, 109)

52. Msg (C/NOFORN-GDS-80), OUSAIRA Vientiane to COMUSMACV, 7AF, et al., Subj: Air Operations in Barrel Roll (U), 050926Z Nov 72. (CMR S-807, 109)

53. Msg (C-GDS-80), OUSAIRA Vientiane to 7/13AF, Subj: ROE MR IV Laos (U), 151530Z Nov 72. (CMR S-807,109)

54. Msg (C-GDS-80), 7AF to AIG 789, Subj: OPS Supplement 105 to 7AF OPORD 71-17 (U), 270715Z Nov 72. (CMR S-951, 005)

55. Msg (C-GDS-80), 7AF to AIG 789, Subj: Operational Supplement 108 to 7AF OPORD 71-17 (U), 140405Z Dec 72. (CMR S-951, 005)

56. Msg (C/NOFORN-GDS-80), OUSAIRA Vientiane to MACV/MACDO-222 and 7AF, Subj: No Bomb Line (U), 191000Z Dec 72. (CMR S-799, 019)

57. Msg (C-GDS-80), 7AF to AIG 789, Subj: OPS Supplement 111 to 7AF OPORD 71-17 (U), 250551Z Dec 72. (CMR S-807, 111)

58. Msg (C-GDS-80), 7AF to AIG 789, Subj: OPS Supplement 112 to 7AF OPORD 71-17 (U), 250640Z Dec 72. (CMR S-807, 111)

59. Msg (C/NOFORN-GDS-80), OUSAIRA Vientiane to COMUSMACV, 7/13AF, et al., Subj: Air Operations in Barrel Roll (U), 271215Z Dec 72. (CMR S-807, 108)

60. Msg (C/NOFORN-GDS-80), OUSAIRA Vientiane to 7/13AF and 474TFW, Subj: Instrument Delivery (ID) Areas in Barrel Roll (U), 131130Z Nov 72. (CMR S-807, 109)

61. Msg (C-GDS-80), OUSAIRA Vientiane to 7AF MACDO 222, 7AF TACC, et al., Subj: Beacon Delivery Zone (U), 271331Z Dec 72. (CMR S-807, 108)

62. Msg (C-GDS-80), OUSAIRA Vientiane to 7AF MACDO 222, 7AF TACC, et al., Subj: Beacon Delivery Zone (U), 312230Z Dec 72. (CMR S-807, 110)

63. Msg (C-GDS-80), OUSAIRA Vientiane to 7AF MACDO 222, ARR INTEL SUKT Laos, et al., Subj: Armed Recce (U), 290610Z Dec 72. (CMR S-807, 108)

Msg (C-GDS-80), 7AF to AIG 789, Subj: OPS Supplement 117 to 7AF OPORD 71-17 (U), 300140Z Dec 72. (CMR S-807, 111)

Msg (C-GDS-81), 7AF to AIG 789, Subj: OPS Supplement 118 to 7AF OPORD 71-17 (U), 051630Z Jan 73. (CMR S-951, 004)

Msg (C-GDS-81), 7AF to AIG 789, Subj: OPS Supplement 119 to 7AF OPORD 71-17 (U), 081731Z Jan 73. (CMR S-807, 111)

64. Msg (C-GDS-81), 7AF to AIG 789, Subj: OPS Supplement 125 to 7AF OPORD 71-17 (U), 180145Z Jan 73. (CMR S-951, 004)

65. Msg (TS-XGDS-3), JCS to CINCPAC and CINCSAC, Subj: SEAsia Operating Authorities--Cease-Fire in RVN and NVN (U), 270657Z Jan 73. (CMR TS-222, 024)

66. Msg (C-GDS-81), 7AF to AIG 789, Subj: OPS Supplement 129 to 7AF OPORD 71-17 (U), 270750Z Jan 73. (CMR S-951, 004)

67. 7AF OPORD 71-17 (S/NOFORN-XCL-3), p. IV-15.

68. Msg (C-GDS-81), 7AF to AIG 789, Subj: OPS Supplement 131 to 7AF OPORD 71-17 (U), 300945Z Jan 73. (CMR S-951, 003)

    Msg (C-GDS-81), 7AF to AIG 789, Subj: OPS Supplement 132 to 7AF OPORD 71-17 (U), 311350Z Jan 73. (CMR S-951, 003)

69. Msg (C-GDS-81), 7AF to AIG 789, Subj: OPS Supplement 133 to 7AF OPORD 71-17 (U), 030520Z Feb 73. (CMR S-951, 003)

70. Msg (C-GDS-81), USSAG/7AF to AIG 789, Subj: OPS Supplement 137 to 7AF OPORD 71-17 (U), 151125Z Feb 73. (CMR S-951, 002)

    Msg (C-GDS-81), USSAG/7AF to AIG 789, Subj: OPS Supplement 136 to 7AF OPORD 71-17 (U), 150955Z Feb 73. (CMR S-951, 002)

71. Msg (TS-XGDS-3), JCS to CINCPAC and CINCSAC, Subj: Operating Authorities--Laos (U), 212337Z Feb 73, retransmitted by CINCPAC to USSAG/7AF in 220141Z Feb 73. (CMR TS-222, 024)

72. Msg (C-GDS-81), USSAG/7AF to AIG 789, Subj: OPS Supplement 139 to 7AF OPORD 71-17 (U), 060855Z Mar 73. (CMR S-951, 002)

73. Msg (TS-XGDS-3), JCS to CINCPAC and CINCSAC, Subj: SE Asia Operating Authorities (U), 291610Z Mar 73. (CMR TS-222, 027)

74. Msg (C-GDS-81), USSAG/7AF to AIG 789, Subj: OPS Supplement 143 to 7AF OPORD 71-17 (U), 311101Z Mar 73. (CMR S-951, 001)

75. Msg (TS-XGDS-3), JCS to CINCPAC and CINCSAC, Subj: Air Operations--Laos (S), 151925Z Apr 73. (CMR TS-222, 011)

76. Msg (C-GDS-81), USSAG/7AF to AIG 789, Subj: OPS Supplement 150 to 7AF OPORD 71-17 (U), 151020Z May 73. (CMR S-951, 001)

    Msg (C-GDS-81), USSAG/7AF to AIG 789, Subj: OPS Supplement 152 to 7AF OPORD 71-17 (U), 071100Z Jan 73. (CMR S-951, 001)

77. Msg (C-GDS-79), JCS to CINCPAC and CINCSAC, Subj: Stop Bombing Legislation (U), 062009Z Jul 73. (CMR S-951, 008)

78. Msg (S-GDS-83), USSAG/7AF to AIG 789, Subj: SE Asia Operating Authorities (U), 080915Z Aug 73. (CMR TS-222, 033)

79. Msg (TS-XGDS-3), JCS to CINCPAC and CINCSAC, Subj: Revised SE Asia Operating Authorities (U), 142336Z Aug 73. (CMR TS-222, 045)

80. Msg (S-GDS-83), CINCPAC to COMUSSAG/7AF, Subj: Operating Authorities (U), 150047Z Sep 73. (CMR TS-222, 034)

81. Msg (S-GDS-83), JCS to CINCPAC and CINCSAC, Subj: Laos Reconnaissance Overflight (C), 152325Z Sep 73. (CMR TS-222, 034)

82. Msg (S-GDS-83), JCS to CINCPAC and CINCSAC, Subj: Laos Reconnaissance (U), 212346Z Sep 73. (CMR TS-222, 038)

83. Project CHECO Report (S-GDS-83), <u>Air Operations in the Khmer Republic--1 Dec 1971-15 Aug 1973</u> (U), 15 Apr 74, p. 10. (Hereafter cited as <u>Air Ops in Khmer Republic</u>.) Material used is Confidential.

84. Msg (TS-XGDS-3), JCS to CINCPAC and CINCSAC, Subj: SE Asia Operating Authorities--Cease-Fire in RVN and NVN (U), 270657Z Jan 73. (CMR TS-222, 024)

85. Air Ops in Khmer Republic (S), p. 18. Material used is Confidential.

86. Msg (TS-XGDS-3), JCS to CINCPAC and CINCSAC, Subj: US Air Operations in Cambodia (C), 052223Z Mar 73. (CMR TS-222, 029)

    Msg (TS-XGDS-3), JCS to CINCPAC and CINCSAC, Subj: Air Operations in Cambodia (U), 081525Z Mar 73. (CMR TS-222, 029)

    Msg (TS-XGDS-3), CINCPAC to JCS/CJCS and COMUSSAG/7AF, Subj: Air Operations in Cambodia (U), 090223Z Mar 73. (CMR TS-222, 029)

    Msg (TS-XGDS-3), BG Cleland, CHMEDT, to Gen Vogt, COMUSSAG/7AF, Subj: Air Operations Cambodia (U), 090912Z Mar 73. (CMR TS-222, 029)

    Msg (C-GDS-81), 7AF to 8TFW, 354TFW, et al., Subj: ROE--Khmer Republic-Freedom Deal (U), 091230Z Mar 73. (CMR TS-212, 040)

    Air Ops in Khmer Republic (S), p. 22. Material used is Secret.

87. Msg (C-GDS-81), USDAO, Phnom Penh, to USSAG/7AF (TMO/DO), Subj: New Freedom Deal Boundaries, Cat A and B LOC Revalidation, and Requested Jettison Areas (U), 310316Z Mar 73. (CMR TS-218, 138)

88. Air Ops in Khmer Republic (S), p. 36. Material used is Confidential.

89. Msg (S-GDS-83), CHMEDTC, Phnom Penh, to CINCPAC and COMUSSAG/7AF, Subj: Air Operations Cambodia (U), 011551Z Apr 73. (CMR TS-222, 030)

    Msg (S-GDS-83), AFSSO, NKP RTAFB, to SSO, Phnom Penh, and SSO, Camp Smith, Hawaii, Subj: Air Operations Cambodia (U), 030505Z Apr 73. (CMR TS-222, 036)

90. Msg (S-GDS-83), USSAG/7AF to 7ACCS and 23TASS/OLI, Subj: Special Military Air Sector (U), 051230Z Apr 73. (CMR TS-222, 030)

    Msg (S-GDS-83), USSAG/7AF to CINCPAC, Subj: Khmer Air Operations (U), 060920Z Apr 73. (CMR TS-222, 030)

91. Msg (S-GDS-83), BG Cleland, CHMEDTC, to Gen Vogt, COMUSSAG/7AF, Subj: Special Mekong Air Sector (U), 041209Z Apr 73. (CMR TS-222, 030)

92. Msg (S-GDS-83), AFSSO, NKP RTAFB, to SSO, Phnom Penh, and SSO, Camp Smith, Hawaii, Subj: Air Operations Cambodia (U), 030505Z Apr 73. (CMR TS-222, 036)

93. Msg (U), USSAG/7AF to 8TFW, 354TFW, et al., Subj: ROE--Khmer Republic (U), 070850Z Apr 73. (CMR TS-218, 130)

    Msg (C-GDS-81), USSAG/7AF to AIG 789, Subj: OPS Supplement 147 to 7AF OPORD 71-17 (U), 070851Z Apr 73. (CMR TS-218, 135)

94. Msg (C-GDS-81), USSAG/7AF to AIG 789, Subj: OPS Supplement 149 to 7AF OPORD 71-17 (U), 141031Z Apr 73. (CMR S-951, 001)

95. Msg (C-GDS-81), USSAG/7AF to AIG 789, Subj: OPS Supplement 148 to 7AF OPORD 71-17 (U), 150545Z Apr 73. (CMR S-951, 001)

96. Msg (S-GDS-83), AFSSO, NKP, to SSO, CINCPAC, Subj: Operational Procedures (U), 170250Z Apr 73. (CMR TS-222, 013)

97. Msg (S-GDS-83), SecState to CINCPAC, CINCSAC, et al., Subj: Proposed Change in Procedures for TACAIR/Gunship Support in Cambodia (U), 171504Z Apr 73. (CMR TS-222, 029)

    Msg (TS-XGDS-3), Adm Moorer, CJCS, to Adm Gayler, CINCPAC, and Gen Meyer, CINCSAC, Subj: SE Asia Operating Authorities (U), 280028Z Apr 73. (CMR TS-222, 030)

98. Msg (S-GDS-83), AFSSO, NKP, to SSO, Phnom Penh, Subj: SE Asia Operating Authorities (U), 281015Z Apr 73. (CMR TS-222, 012)

99. Air Ops in Khmer Republic (S), p. 29. Material used is Confidential.

100. Ibid.

101. Msg (S-GDS-83), SSO, Phnom Penh, to AFSSO, NKP, Subj: Khmer Monthly Validation (U), 270750Z May 73. (CMR TS-222, 014)

   Msg (TS-XGDS-3), Amb Swank, Phnom Penh, to Gen Vogt, COMUSSAG/7AF, Subj: Khmer Monthly Validations (U), 251155Z Jun 73. (CMR TS-222, 011)

102. Msg (C-GDS-81), USSAG/7AF to AIG 789, Subj: OPS Supplement 143 to 7AF OPORD 71-17 (U), 311101Z Mar 73. (CMR S-951, 001)

103. Msg (S-GDS-83), JCS to CINCPAC, Subj: Operations Within RVN Positive Control Area (U), 030142Z Aug 73. (CMR TS-222, 033)

104. Msg (C-GDS-81), USSAG/7AF to AIG 789, Subj: OPS Supplement 153 to 7AF OPORD 71-17 (U), 051100Z Aug 73. (CMR S-951, 001)

105. Msg (C-GDS-81), JCS to CINCPAC and CINCSAC, Subj: U.S. Operations in SE Asia (U), 111309Z Aug 73. (CMR S-951, 001)

106. Msg (S-GDS-83), USSAG/7AF to AmEmb Phnom Penh, Subj: Operating Authorities and Basic Rules of Engagement for KHR Cease-Fire in NVN, RVN, and DMZ, Laos, and Cessation of Combat Activities by U.S. Forces in GKR (U), undated (c. 15 Aug 73). (CMR TS-222, 002)

107. USSAG OPORD 74-91 (S-XGDS-2, Declassify on 31 Dec 88), DOCM, Rules of Engagement--Southeast Asia (U), 1 Feb 74, p. i. (CMR S-986, 155)

## GLOSSARY

| | |
|---|---|
| AAA | antiaircraft artillery |
| ABCCC | airborne battlefield command and control center |
| ADCC | air defense control center |
| AmEmb | American Embassy |
| AOA | air operating authorities |
| AOC | air operations center |
| ASD | Assistant Secretary of Defense |
| | |
| BDZ | beacon delivery zone |
| BR | Barrel Roll |
| | |
| CAS | close air support |
| CHMEDTC | Chief, Military Equipment Delivery Team, Cambodia |
| CINCPAC | Commander in Chief, Pacific Command |
| CINCPACAF | Commander in Chief, Pacific Air Forces |
| CJCS | Chairman, Joint Chiefs of Staff |
| COC | combat operations center |
| COIN | counterinsurgency |
| COMUSMACV | Commander, U.S. Military Assistance Command, Vietnam |
| COMUSSAG | Commander, U.S. Support Activities Group |
| | |
| DMZ | demilitarized zone |
| DRV | Democratic Republic of Vietnam (the government of North Vietnam) |
| | |
| FAC | forward air controller |
| FAG | forward air guide |
| FANK | Forces Armees Nationale Khmer (Cambodian Army) |
| frag | fragmentary order |
| | |
| GKR | Government of Khmer Republic |
| GVN | Government of (South) Vietnam |
| | |
| IFF | identification friend or foe |
| IFR | instrument flight rules |
| | |
| JCRC | Joint Casualty Resolution Center |
| JCS | Joint Chiefs of Staff |
| | |
| KAF | Khmer Air Force |
| KDASC | Khmer Direct Air Support Center |
| KI | Khmer insurgents |

| | |
|---|---|
| LOC | line of communication |
| LORAN | long range airborne navigation |
| MedEvac | medical evacuation |
| MR | military region |
| NGFS | naval gunfire support |
| NM | nautical mile |
| NVA | North Vietnamese Army |
| NVN | North Vietnam |
| OUSAIRA | Office of U.S. Air Attache |
| PACOM | Pacific Command |
| PCA | positive control area |
| PCZ | positive control zone |
| PMDL | provisional military demarcation line |
| POL | petroleum, oil, and lubricants |
| POW | prisoner of war |
| PRC | People's Republic of China |
| PSYOP | psychological operations |
| RCA | riot control agent |
| RLAF | Royal Lao Air Force |
| RLG | Royal Lao Government |
| ROE | rules of engagement |
| RTAF | Royal Thai Air Force |
| RVN | Republic of Vietnam |
| RVNAF | Republic of Vietnam Armed Forces |
| SAM | surface-to-air missile |
| SAR | search and rescue |
| SEA | Southeast Asia |
| SecDef | Secretary of Defense |
| SIGINT | signal intelligence |
| SL | Steel Tiger |
| SMAS | Special Mekong Air Sector |
| SOA | special operating area |
| SPIN | special instruction |
| SSZ | specified strike zone |
| TACAIR | tactical air (forces, strikes, support, etc) |
| TACC | tactical air control center |
| TIC | troops in contact |
| USSAG/7AF | U.S. Support Activities Group/Seventh Air Force |

| | |
|---|---|
| VC | Viet Cong, Vietnamese communist(s) |
| VFR | visual flight rules |
| VNAF | Vietnamese (South) Air Force |

## DISTRIBUTION

SECRETARY OF THE AIR FORCE
- SAF/AA .................... 1
- SAF/LLV ................... 1
- SAF/OI .................... 1
- SAF/US .................... 1

HEADQUARTERS USAF
- AF/CHO .................... 2
- AF/DP ..................... 1
- AF/IG ..................... 1
  - OSI/IVOA ................ 1
  - SPO ..................... 1
- AF/IS
  - INDOC ................... 1
  - INZA .................... 1
  - INTA .................... 1
  - INYXX ................... 1
- AF/KRCCT .................. 1
- AF/LG
  - LGX ..................... 1
  - LGTT .................... 1
- AF/NB ..................... 1
- AF/PR
  - PRC ..................... 1
  - PRP ..................... 1
- AF/RD
  - RDQ ..................... 1
  - RDQPC ................... 1
  - RDR ..................... 1
- AF/XO
  - XOCD .................... 1
  - XOCC .................... 1
  - XOCRC ................... 1
  - XOOG .................... 1
  - XOOSLC .................. 1
  - XOOSN ................... 1
  - XOOSR ................... 1
  - XOOSS ................... 1
  - XOOSZ ................... 1
  - XOXAA ................... 5
  - XOXFCM .................. 1
  - XOOSW ................... 1

MAJOR COMMANDS
- ADC
  - DOT ..................... 1
  - 25AD/DOI ................ 1
- AFSC
  - ADTC/CCN ................ 1
  - ADTC/DLOSL .............. 1
  - AFATL/DL ................ 1
  - ASD/RWR ................. 1
  - ESD/YWA ................. 1
  - HO ...................... 1
  - RADC/DOT ................ 1
  - XRPA .................... 1
- MAC
  - DOO ..................... 1
  - INX ..................... 1
  - HO ...................... 1
  - 60MAW/INX ............... 1
  - 317TAW/IN ............... 1
  - ARRS/DOX ................ 1
- PACAF
  - DC ...................... 1
  - HO ...................... 6
  - LG ...................... 1
  - OA ...................... 1
  - 5AF/DO .................. 1
    - HO .................... 1
    - XP .................... 1
  - 13AF/HO ................. 1
  - 8TFW/DO ................. 1
  - 18TFW/IN ................ 1
  - 51CW(T)/DO .............. 1
- SAC
  - HO ...................... 1
  - IN ...................... 1
  - LG ...................... 1
  - NRI (STINFO Library) .... 1
- TAC
  - DOC ..................... 1
  - DREA .................... 1
  - IN ...................... 1
  - XPS ..................... 1

141

TAC (Cont'd)
   1SOW/IN........................ 1
   23TFW/IN....................... 1
   27TFW/IN....................... 1
   35TFW/IN....................... 1
   366TFW/IN...................... 1
   USAFTAWC/IN.................... 1
   USAFTFWC/TA.................... 1
   USAFAGOS/EDAC.................. 1

USAFE
   DOA............................ 1
   DOLO........................... 1
   DOOW........................... 1
   XPX............................ 1
   3AF/DO......................... 1

USAFE (Cont'd)
   16AF/DO........................ 1
   513TAW/DOI..................... 1

   USAFSOS/EDSL................... 1
   USAFSS/AFEWC/SUR).............. 2

SEPARATE OPERATING AGENCIES
   DMAAC/PR....................... 1
   3825Acad Svs Gp
      AUL/LSE-69-108............. 2
      AFSHRC/HOTI................ 2
   Analytic Svs, Inc.............. 1
   AFFDL/FES/CDIC................. 1
   USAFA/DFSLB.................... 1

MILITARY DEPARTMENTS, UNIFIED AND SPECIFIED COMMANDS, AND JOINT STAFFS
   CINCPAC/J34 (Reference Library).................................. 1
   CINCPACFLT (32).................................................. 1
   COMUSKOREA (Attn: J-3)........................................... 1
   COMUSTDC/J3...................................................... 1
   USCINCEUR/ECJB................................................... 1
   CINCLANT/CL...................................................... 1
   Chief, Naval Operations, Bureau of Naval Personnel (Pers-63)..... 1
   Commandant, Marine Corps/ABQ..................................... 1
   Department of the Army/ASM-D..................................... 1
   Joint Chiefs of Staff/Chief, Pacific Division, OJCS.............. 1
   Secretary of Defense/OASD/SA..................................... 1
   USREDCOM (Attn: RCJ3)............................................ 1
   MAAG-CHINA/MGXO.................................................. 1
   Hq Allied Forces Northern Europe, Air Deputy-AF North............ 1

SCHOOLS
   Senior USAF Rep, National War College (NWCLB-CR)................. 1
   Senior USAF Rep, Armed Forces Staff College...................... 1
   Senior USAF Rep, Industrial College of the Armed Forces.......... 1
   Senior USAF Rep, U.S. Naval Amphibious School.................... 1
   Senior USAF Rep, U.S. Marine Corps Education Center.............. 1
   Senior USAF Rep, U.S. Naval War College.......................... 1
   Senior USAF Rep, U.S. Army War College........................... 1
   Senior USAF Rep, U.S. Army C&G Staff College..................... 1
   Senior USAF Rep, U.S. Army Infantry School....................... 1
   Senior USAF Rep, USA JFK Center for Military Assistance.......... 1
   Senior USAF Rep, U.S. Army Field Artillery School................ 1
   Senior USAF Rep, U.S. Liaison Office, Hq AFCENT.................. 1
   Senior USAF Rep, U.S. Army Armor School, Comd & Staff Dep........ 1